paradise served

SOUTH FLORIDA'S CULINARY DESTINATION

JUNIOR LEAGUE OF GREATER FORT LAUDERDALE

paradise served

SOUTH FLORIDA'S CULINARY DESTINATION

Published by
Junior League of Greater Fort Lauderdale, Inc.
704 Southeast First Street
Fort Lauderdale, Florida 33301
Phone 954.462.1350
Fax 954.462.1677
www.juniorleagueftl.org

Copyright © 2009 by
Junior League of Greater Fort Lauderdale, Inc.

Photography Copyright © by Andrew Meade

Chairs: Rochelle Darman, Lori Ebinger Sullivan

Library of Congress Control Number:
2008930261
ISBN: 978-0-9604158-3-0

Edited, Designed, and Produced by
Favorite Recipes® Press
An imprint of

FRP.

a wholly owned subsidary of
Southwestern/Great American, Inc.
P.O. Box 305142
Nashville, Tennessee 37230
800.358.0560

Art Direction and Book Design: Starletta Polster
Project Editor: Nicki Pendleton Wood

Manufactured in the United States of America
First Printing: 2009   10,000 copies

contents

our mission

The Junior League of Greater Fort Lauderdale is an organization of women committed to promoting voluntarism, developing the potential of women, and improving the community through effective action and leadership of trained volunteers.

who we are

We are the Junior League of Greater Fort Lauderdale, a group of diverse women who share a feeling of responsibility toward our community and want to play a role in shaping its future. We are business professionals, wives, mothers, grandmothers, aunts, sisters, students, trainers, fund-raisers, and community activists. We are different ages and different races and have come from different places. We call South Florida home, and we all joined the Junior League because we care about improving our community. We have trained thousands of women to address community needs and to take on leadership roles at every level.

The Junior League of Greater Fort Lauderdale was founded in 1937 as the Fort Lauderdale Junior Service League to provide the community with willing volunteers in civic and child welfare work. In 1959 the Junior League of Greater Fort Lauderdale became a member of the Association of Junior Leagues International, an organization of autonomous leagues throughout the United States, Canada, Great Britain, and Mexico. The Junior League of Greater Fort Lauderdale is now more than seven hundred members strong and growing.

We support more than fifty local organizations—many of which we founded—with our time, resources, and leadership. We continue to research community needs and follow through with real-time action and large-scale projects based on our findings. Projects are supported with financial, administrative, and volunteer assistance until they become self-sufficient. Read on and you will learn about projects created by the Junior League of Greater Fort Lauderdale that now stand as landmarks and legacies in this community.

Cover photo: Grapefruit Daiquiris, recipe page 48; Caramel Fruit Dip, recipe page 143

Photo, left: Neopolitas, recipe page 155; Key Lime Bites, recipe page 157; Chippy Dippy Bars, recipe page 153

JUNIOR LEAGUE OF
GREATER FORT LAUDERDALE
Women building better communities

Welcome to Paradise!

Expressions. We all have our favorites . . . . everything from "The early bird gets the worm" to "A picture is worth a thousand words!"

Well, I've heard "Good things come in threes." Now I know it's true, as I welcome you to our slice of paradise and our third cookbook, *Paradise Served*. This eclectic collection of recipes now joins our two other popular titles, *Sunny Side Up* and *Made in the Shade*, which is the official cookbook of the City of Fort Lauderdale.

Paradise Served—we love this title! The word "paradise" perfectly describes our sun-drenched beaches and endless waterways—a big city with rich history, charm, and sophistication brimming with small, unique neighborhoods and people as beautiful as the weather. And the word "served" embodies our Junior League's commitment to service in Greater Fort Lauderdale—as well as being a tribute to the delicious recipes that are served from our trio of cookbooks.

Another popular expression is "Too many cooks spoil the broth." Well, that couldn't be further from the truth in this case! In all, more than four hundred of our Junior League members, families, friends, community leaders, and local celebrities contributed to *Paradise Served*—either by submitting a recipe or by testing one. It was a colossal community effort that you will taste on every page.

Do "More hands make lighter work"? Yes, they do! Since 1937, the Junior League of Greater Fort Lauderdale has brought women together in the spirit of voluntarism, giving countless volunteer hours of invaluable hands-on planning, project development, training, and fund-raising in all facets of community stewardship. We take pride in the instrumental role we've had in founding community treasures, such as Jack and Jill Children's Center and the Museum of Discovery and Science, and our most recent collaboration that assists youth as they transition from the foster care system to adulthood. Whether it's lending a helping hand or leading the way, we are women building better communities.

Time really does fly when you're having fun! It seems as if we blinked and our first seventy years are behind us. Blink again and *Paradise Served* is here and ready to take its rightful place on kitchen counters and bookshelves in Fort Lauderdale and far beyond, with everyone from casual collectors to aficionados!

Thank you for taking our paradise home with you and sharing what you've served. Your support of *Paradise Served* ensures our rich legacy will continue for generations to come!

All's well that ends well,

Audrey Ring

Audrey Ring
Board President

professional credits

April L. Alder—Food stylist. April is a Fort Lauderdale native. She earned her degree in Culinary Arts from the National Center for Hospitality Studies at Sullivan University in Louisville, Kentucky. April perfected her craft working as a caterer, private chef, and at the Four Seasons Resort in Palm Beach, The Terrace Restaurant, and the Louisville landmark Hasenour's Restaurant. April and her husband, Wayne, and two children reside in Parkland, Florida, where she teaches private cooking classes that focus on the flavors and presentation of food. On her experience with *Paradise Served*, April says, "It is an honor to be part of a project for the Junior League of Greater Fort Lauderdale that raises funds that truly make a difference in our community."

Marlene Goldfarb—Set stylist. Marlene graduated with honors from the Art Institute of Fort Lauderdale with a double major in Advertising Design and Fashion Illustration. She began her career in visual merchandising and store design with Macy's and Saks Fifth Avenue. Travel in her home country of the Republic of Panama inspired her personal sense of design to create visual impact for upscale retailers. Upon her return to Miami, she entered the world of television commercials for Publix Super Markets and from there she became a set decorator and photography stylist. Her work is featured in catalogues including Linens 'n Things, ABC Distributing, and Charles Keith; resort advertising for Marriott, Paradissus, and Fountainbleau; and real estate advertising for Midtown Miami, The Beach Club, and Turnberry. Her latest project is as set decorator on the hit Food Network cooking show *Simply Delicioso* with Ingrid Hoffmann.

Andrew Meade—Photographer. Andrew Meade has been working as a professional photographer for the past eight years, specializing in still life and food photography. Some of his clients include the Food Network, Tribune Publishing, *DiningOut* magazine, Ritz Carlton Resorts & Spas, and The Diplomat Resort & Spa. Andrew resides in Fort Lauderdale and his latest work can be seen in Ingrid Hoffmann's first cookbook, entitled *Simply Delicioso*. Visit his Web site at www.andrewmeade.com.

our legacy at a glance

Jack and Jill Children's Center: Founded in 1942 to provide child care for the children of working mothers whose husbands were at war. The center now works to break the cycle of poverty for children of low-income, working families in Broward County through family-oriented child-care services, family intervention, and support.

Henderson Mental Health: Founded in 1953 to address the lack of public, affordable psychiatric and casework services to the families of Broward County. The center is now the oldest and largest behavioral health care provider in South Florida.

Museum of Art: Founded in 1958, the art museum was housed in a renovated hardware store on Las Olas Boulevard. Since its founding, the Museum of Art has grown into a major community cultural resource marked by a commitment to quality, inclusion, and collaboration with a collection of 6,200 paintings, drawings, and sculpture.

Volunteer Broward: Formed in 1969 as a clearinghouse for recruiting and interviewing volunteers to match them with nonprofit agency positions. Today, Volunteer Broward refers individuals and groups to more than six hundred nonprofit organizations in the county.

Museum of Discovery and Science: Founded as a children's learning center in 1969, the Discovery Center was originally a small hands-on children's museum. Today, it is an 11,000-square-foot exhibit space with a five-story-high IMAX Theater, all designed to provide experiential pathways to lifelong learning in science for children and adults.

Kids in Distress: Founded in 1976 and is dedicated to the prevention of child abuse, the preservation of the family, and the care and treatment of abused and neglected children. Kids in Distress is a temporary "home away from home" for children who are removed from their families because of abuse. Kids in Distress offers shelter and therapeutic and group home care.

SOS Children's Village: Opened in 1993, SOS Children's Village was the only community of its kind in the United States. Designed to serve abused and abandoned foster children who are unlikely to be adopted or reunited with family members, these children live with caregivers in homes that were made possible through eight acres of property acquired with the assistance of the Junior League.

OUR House: Founded in 1994, OUR House is a safe, warm, and friendly place, where children can have supervised weekly visits with their estranged parents in a home-like environment. OUR House families are referred by the court system or Department of Children and Families for supervised visitations and/or safe exchanges while usually receiving other interventions.

Susan B. Anthony Recovery Center: Founded in 1995, the center was designed to address the need for residential treatment services for families involved in substance addiction and in the child welfare system and is intended to allow families to stay intact while completing the recovery process. The Junior League was responsible for the initial project development and the creation of the capital campaign.

a glimpse at our future

In 2005, the Junior League of Greater Fort Lauderdale recognized that when Broward County's foster youth turned eighteen, they would "age out" of the foster care system, asked to leave their current foster homes and left to learn to live on their own, most without any support. As a result, many of these teens were dropping out of high school, becoming dependent on welfare, or becoming homeless, pregnant, or involved with the criminal justice system.

Identifying this as a problem in the community that needed attention, the Junior League researched this issue locally and nationally. In 2007, they began the development of a Transitional Independent Living (TIL) Resource Center. The goal of the TIL Resource Center is to change the lives of Broward County's dependent and emancipated youth by making services more readily available to them in order to promote self-sufficient and productive members of the community.

To achieve this goal, the Junior League has partnered with various Broward County agencies to develop an Independent Living Skills Program. This initiative will provide real world living experiences for foster youth age seventeen prior to emancipation, and to emancipated foster youth ages eighteen to twenty-three, and will establish a centrally located Resource Center where the teens can access a variety of resources (for example, life coaches, employment, education, and housing specialists) and learn and practice independent living and social skills.

breakfast & breads served

P.S.

Planning an outdoor soiree? Don't get blown away by the breeze! Use large shells as a creative way to windproof your party by holding down paper plates and napkins. Keep tablecloths steady by securing a pair of magnets on each corner or by using tablecloth clamps.

sunrise frittata

MAKES 4 SERVINGS

6 eggs	1/4 cup fresh salsa
1/2 cup half-and-half	1/4 cup chopped fresh parsley
1 cup (4 ounces) shredded Gouda cheese	Salt and pepper to taste
1/2 cup bacon bits	2 tablespoons butter
1 tomato, chopped	

Combine the eggs, half-and-half, cheese, bacon bits, tomato, salsa, parsley, salt and pepper in a bowl and mix well. Melt the butter in a nonstick 9-inch skillet over medium heat. Pour in the egg mixture. Cook for 2 minutes, then scrape the bottom of the pan with a spatula to allow the uncooked egg mixture to run underneath. Preheat the broiler. Place the pan under the broiler when three-fourths of the eggs are cooked and the top is still runny. Broil for 3 to 5 minutes to cook the top. Remove the frittata to a serving platter. Cut into wedges to serve.

Photo, page 10: *Sun Your Cinnamon Buns, recipe page 20*

mushroom and spinach strata

MAKES 10 TO 12 SERVINGS

6 to 8 cups sliced mushrooms

1/4 cup (1/2 stick) unsalted butter

1/4 cup sun-dried tomatoes, finely chopped

1/4 teaspoon thyme

2 teaspoons basil

1/4 cup chopped onions

1/4 cup (1/2 stick) butter

16 ounces chopped frozen spinach, thawed, drained and squeezed dry

1/3 cup crumbled crisp-cooked bacon

1/3 cup Parmesan cheese

8 ounces ricotta cheese

12 croissants, cut into halves horizontally

1 cup (4 ounces) shredded mozzarella cheese

6 eggs

2 cups milk

1 teaspoon salt

1/2 teaspoon white pepper

1/4 teaspoon nutmeg

1/3 cup Parmesan cheese

3 tablespoons butter, melted

Sauté the mushrooms in 1/4 cup butter in a skillet until tender. Add the sun-dried tomatoes, thyme and basil and set aside. Sauté the onions in 1/4 cup butter in a skillet until tender. Stir in the spinach, bacon, 1/3 cup Parmesan cheese and the ricotta cheese. Grease a 9x13-inch baking pan. Line the bottom with eight croissant halves, crust side down. Spoon the mushroom mixture over the croissant halves. Top with the remaining croissants. Sprinkle with the mozzarella cheese. Beat the eggs, milk, salt, white pepper and nutmeg in a bowl. Pour over the layers. Press down to moisten all layers. Refrigerate for 24 hours.

Preheat the oven to 375 degrees. Sprinkle with 1/3 cup Parmesan cheese and drizzle with 3 tablespoons butter. Bake for 45 minutes or until puffed and brown.

brunch casserole

1 pound bulk pork sausage
1 (8-count) can refrigerator crescent rolls
2 cups (8 ounces) shredded mozzarella cheese
4 eggs

3/4 cup milk
1/4 teaspoon salt
1/8 teaspoon pepper

Preheat the oven to 425 degrees. Brown the sausage in a skillet, stirring until crumbly; drain and set aside. Grease a 9x13-inch baking pan. Line with the crescent rolls, pressing the perforations to seal. Layer the sausage and cheese over the dough. Beat the eggs, milk, salt and pepper in a bowl until well combined. Pour over the layers. Bake for 15 minutes or until set. Let stand for 5 minutes. Cut into squares and serve immediately.

swedish pancakes

MAKES 4 TO 6 SERVINGS

4 eggs
2 cups milk
1/4 cup sugar
1 1/2 teaspoons salt

1 1/4 cups all-purpose flour
1/2 cup (1 stick) butter
Additional butter
Syrup

Beat the eggs, milk, sugar, salt and flour until well blended. The batter will be thin. Heat a large skillet over medium-high heat. Add 1 tablespoon of the butter. Heat until the butter sizzles. Add 1/4 to 1/3 cup of the batter to the pan, tilting to cover the bottom. Cook for 1 to 2 minutes or until golden brown. Turn and cook for 1 to 2 minutes longer or until golden brown. Repeat with the remaining batter. Serve immediately with butter and syrup.

For a special occasion, serve two or three pancakes topped with a scoop of vanilla ice cream, sliced fresh strawberries, and a dollop of whipped cream.

crème brûlée french toast

MAKES 6 TO 8 SERVINGS

1/2 cup (1 stick) unsalted butter
1 cup packed brown sugar
2 tablespoons corn syrup
1 loaf challah
5 eggs

1 1/2 cups half-and-half
1 teaspoon vanilla extract
1/4 teaspoon salt
1 teaspoon Grand Marnier (optional)

Melt the butter with the brown sugar and corn syrup in a small heavy saucepan over medium heat, stirring until smooth. Pour into a 9x13-inch baking pan. Cut six 1-inch-thick slices from the center of the loaf. Trim the crusts, if desired. Arrange the bread slices in a single layer in the baking dish, pressing to fit all the slices if necessary.

Beat the eggs, half-and-half, vanilla, salt and liqueur in a bowl until well combined. Pour evenly over the bread. Refrigerate, covered, for 8 to 24 hours.

Let stand until room temperature. Preheat the oven to 350 degrees. Bake for 35 to 40 minutes or until the bread is puffed and the edges are golden brown. Invert each slice using a spatula to serve.

heavenly hash browns

MAKES 4 TO 6 SERVINGS

1 (30-ounce) package frozen hash brown potatoes
1/2 cup (1 stick) butter
2 cups (8 ounces) shredded Cheddar cheese

2 cups (8 ounces) grated Parmesan cheese
Additional butter
Paprika

Preheat the oven to 350 degrees. Combine the potatoes, 1/2 cup butter, the Cheddar cheese and Parmesan cheese in a bowl and mix well. Spread in a greased 9x13-inch baking dish. Dot with additional butter. Sprinkle with paprika. Bake for 1 1/2 hours.

Did you know that the watermelon's origin can be traced back to the Kalahari Desert in Africa? The watermelon is actually a vegetable and is related to cucumbers, pumpkins, and squash. Florida led the U.S. in watermelon production in 2006 with 835 million pounds.

twigs and berries granola

MAKES 6 QUARTS

8 cups rolled oats	3/4 cup honey
3 cups soy nuts	1 teaspoon vanilla
2 cups unsalted sunflower seeds	3/4 cup packed brown sugar
1 cup almonds	1/2 teaspoon nutmeg
1 cup cashews	1/2 teaspoon cinnamon
1 1/2 cups unsalted pumpkin seeds	1/2 cup dried cranberries or raisins
3 cups unsweetened shredded coconut	1/2 cup dried apricots or dates
1 cup grapeseed oil	

Preheat the oven to 250 degrees. Combine the oats, soy nuts, sunflower seeds, almonds, cashews, pumpkin seeds and coconut in a large bowl and mix well. Combine the grapeseed oil, honey and vanilla in a small bowl and mix well. Sprinkle the brown sugar, nutmeg and cinnamon over the oat mixture and mix well. Pour the oil mixture over the oat mixture and stir to coat. Spread the mixture in a roasting pan. Bake for 25 minutes, stirring every 10 minutes. Add the cranberries and apricots and bake for 5 minutes longer. Spread the mixture on foil, covering with additional foil. Cool completely.

melon with mint

1 watermelon
1 honeydew melon
1 cantaloupe
Juice of 2 limes

10 to 12 fresh mint leaves
4 slices bacon, crisp-cooked and
crumbled (optional)

Scoop out the watermelon, honeydew melon and cantaloupe with a melon baller into a large serving bowl. Add the lime juice and toss to coat. Stack the mint leaves and roll into a cigar shape. Slice into strips. Add to the melon mixture and toss gently. Top with the bacon. Serve cool (not cold) or at room temperature.

perfect pineapple bake

1/2 cup (1 stick) butter
1 cup sugar
4 eggs

1 (20-ounce) can crushed pineapple
8 slices bread, cut into cubes

Preheat oven to 350 degrees. Beat the butter and sugar in a bowl until fluffy and well combined. Add the eggs and mix well. Stir in the undrained pineapple. Fold in the bread cubes. Spoon into a greased 9-inch baking dish. Bake for 1 1/2 hours.

beachside banana bread

2 to 3 bananas, mashed

1/2 cup (1 stick) butter

1 egg

1 1/2 cups all-purpose flour

3/4 cup sugar

1 teaspoon baking soda

1 teaspoon salt

1/2 cup chopped walnuts (optional)

Preheat the oven to 350 degrees. Combine the bananas, butter, egg, flour, sugar, baking soda, salt and walnuts in a bowl, mixing by hand with a spoon. Pour into a loaf pan sprayed with nonstick cooking spray. Bake for 1 hour.

daybreak oatmeal bread

MAKES 2 LOAVES

2 cups boiling water

2 cups quick-cooking or rolled oats

2 tablespoons shortening

2 teaspoons salt

1/2 cup dark molasses

1 envelope active dry yeast

1/2 cup lukewarm water

5 to 6 cups all-purpose flour

Combine 2 cups boiling water and oats in a bowl. Add the shortening and salt and mix well. Let stand to cool. Stir in the molasses. Dissolve the yeast in 1/2 water in a cup. Add to the oats mixture along with 5 cups of the flour, mixing until well combined. Knead or use a dough hook until smooth and elastic, adding additional flour as needed if the dough is sticky. Place in a greased bowl, turning to coat the surface. Let rise, covered, in a warm place until doubled in bulk. Punch down the dough. Divide the dough into two portions. Shape each portion into a loaf and place in two greased loaf pans. Let rise until the dough fills the pans. Preheat the oven to 350 degrees. Bake for 50 minutes. Cool in the pans for 10 minutes. Remove to a wire rack to cool completely.

lucky seven bread

MAKES 12 TO 15 SLICES

1 cup canola oil	**Lucky Seven Options**
2 eggs	2 cups mashed banana
2 cups sugar	2 cups cranberry relish
1 teaspoon vanilla extract	2 cups (12 ounces) chocolate chips, melted
1/2 teaspoon baking soda	2 cups peanut butter
1/2 teaspoon baking powder	1 (15-ounce) can pumpkin
3 cups all-purpose flour	2 cups applesauce
	1 cup shredded zucchini
	Sugar for coating

Preheat the oven to 375 degrees. Beat the canola oil and eggs in a bowl until well combined. Add the sugar and vanilla and beat until light and fluffy. Combine the baking soda, baking powder and flour in a bowl and mix well. Sift the flour mixture into the batter gradually, beating until the batter reaches the consistency of dough.

Select one Lucky Seven option and stir into the batter. The batter will resemble cake batter. Pour into a greased and sugar-coated bundt pan. Bake for 45 to 60 minutes or until the bread tests done. Invert the bread immediately onto a serving platter.

This recipe is from the kitchen of Mayor Larry Gierer.

sun your cinnamon buns

MAKES 6 LARGE SERVINGS

Dough

1 envelope active dry yeast
2 tablespoons sugar
1/2 cup warm water
3 tablespoons plus 1 teaspoon sugar
1/2 cup water
2 eggs
4 cups all-purpose flour
Pinch of salt
1/4 cup vegetable oil

Topping

1/2 cup (1 stick) butter, softened
1 tablespoon cinnamon
1/3 cup packed dark brown sugar
2/3 cup pecans (optional)

For the dough, combine the yeast, 2 tablespoons sugar and 1/2 cup warm water in a large mixing bowl with a wooden spoon, stirring until the yeast is dissolved. Let stand for several minutes or until the mixture is frothy. Add 3 tablespoons plus 1 teaspoon sugar, 1/2 cup water and the eggs and mix well. Add 3 cups of the flour, 1 cup at a time, stirring with a wooden spoon or beating with a mixer fitted with a dough hook. Add the salt, oil and the remaining 1 cup flour. Mix until the dough is smooth and glossy, adding additional flour if the dough is sticky.

Knead the dough on a floured surface until smooth and elastic. Place in a greased bowl, turning to coat the surface. Cover with plastic wrap and let rise in a warm place for several hours or until the dough presses on the plastic wrap.

For the topping, spread the bottom of a 9x13-inch baking pan with the butter. Sprinkle evenly with the cinnamon, brown sugar and pecans.

(continued on the following page)

Filling	**Glaze**
1/2 cup (1 stick) butter, softened	1/4 cup water
7 ounces raisins (optional)	2 cups confectioners' sugar, sifted
1/3 cup pecans (optional)	1 egg white
2 tablespoons dark brown sugar	
1/2 teaspoon cinnamon	

For the filling, roll the dough into a rectangle on a floured surface. Brush evenly with the butter. Sprinkle evenly with raisins, pecans, brown sugar and cinnamon. Roll the dough lengthwise to enclose the filling. Cut into six 1 1/2-inch rounds. Arrange over the topping in the pan. Cover with foil and let rise until full and puffy. Preheat the oven to 350 degrees. Bake for 30 minutes or until firm and golden brown. Invert the pan onto a serving platter and let the gooey goodness drip over the rolls, or use a spatula to serve the rolls from the pan.

For the glaze, combine the water, confectioners' sugar and egg white in a bowl and whisk to blend. Drizzle over the warm buns.

If you are short on time, refrigerate the dough or rolls and bake the next day. The cold will slow the yeast growth. This versatile dough also makes wonderful yeast rolls.

If you are concerned about using raw egg whites, use whites from eggs pasteurized in their shells, which are sold at some specialty food stores, or use an equivalent amount of meringue powder and follow the package directions.

P.S.

Joey McIntyre has been around the block and among the stars! Joey first caught our attention as the youngest member of the best-selling boy band New Kids on the Block. After appearing in the hit show "Boston Public," he went on to dazzle us on the first season of "Dancing with the Stars." While he calls Boston home, he calls South Florida his favorite vacation spot!

the right stuff corn bread

MAKES 12 SERVINGS

1 (8-ounce) package corn bread mix	3/4 cup milk
1 cup self-rising cornmeal	1 jalapeño chile, finely chopped
1 (8-ounce) can cream-style corn	1/2 red bell pepper, finely chopped
2 eggs	

Preheat the oven to 400 degrees. Combine the corn bread mix, cornmeal, corn, eggs, milk, jalapeño chile and bell pepper in a large bowl and mix well. Pour into a greased cast-iron skillet. Bake on the middle oven rack for 25 to 30 minutes or until golden brown.

This recipe is from the kitchen of Joey McIntyre.

irish bread

MAKES 8 TO 10 SERVINGS

1 cup sugar
6 tablespoons butter or margarine, softened
1 egg
1 teaspoon caraway seeds
1 cup raisins

4 cups all-purpose flour
1/4 teaspoon salt
5 teaspoons baking powder
1 1/2 cups milk

Preheat the oven to 325 degrees. Combine the sugar and butter with a whisk or wooden spoon in a bowl until mixed. Add the egg and whisk until well mixed. Stir in the caraway seeds and raisins. Add the flour, salt, baking soda and milk and stir to combine. The mixture will be stiff. Add additional flour and milk if necessary to maintain a workable consistency. Spoon into a 10-inch pie plate or quiche dish. Bake for 1 hour or until the bread tests done and is golden brown. Cool completely before slicing.

pumpkin pie bread

MAKES 2 LOAVES

2 cups all-purpose flour
2 cups granulated sugar
2 (3-ounce) packages vanilla instant pudding mix
1 teaspoon baking soda
1 teaspoon cinnamon
1 or 2 pinches of nutmeg

Pinch of ground cloves
1 1/4 cups vegetable oil
5 eggs
2 cups canned pumpkin
2 cups confectioners' sugar
3 1/3 tablespoons water
1/4 teaspoon vanilla extract

Preheat the oven to 325 degrees. Combine the flour, granulated sugar, pudding mix, baking soda, cinnamon, nutmeg and cloves in a large bowl and mix well. Combine the oil, eggs and pumpkin in a separate bowl and mix well. Add to the dry ingredients, stirring just until combined. Pour into two greased 5x9-inch loaf pans. Bake for 1 1/2 hours or until the loaves test done. Cool in the pan for 15 minutes. Remove to a wire rack to cool completely.

Combine the confectioners' sugar, water and vanilla in a small bowl and whisk until smooth. Drizzle over the loaves, allowing the glaze to run down the sides.

strawberry bread with strawberry spread

MAKES 2 LOAVES AND 1 1/2 CUPS SPREAD

3 cups all-purpose flour
2 cups sugar
1 teaspoon baking soda
1 teaspoon cinnamon

2 (10-ounce) packages frozen sliced strawberries, thawed, drained and 1/2 cup juice reserved
1 cup vegetable oil
4 eggs, beaten
8 ounces cream cheese, softened

Preheat the oven to 350 degrees. Combine the flour, sugar, baking soda, and cinnamon in a large bowl and mix well. Make a well in the center of the flour mixture and add the strawberries, oil and eggs. Stir with a wooden spoon just until combined. Pour into two greased and floured 4x8-inch loaf pans. Bake for 1 hour or until the loaves test done. Cool in the pans for 10 minutes. Remove to a wire rack to cool completely. Mix the cream cheese and the reserved strawberry juice in a bowl until the mixture is of a spreading consistency. Serve with the bread.

pan de yuca

MAKES 15 SERVINGS

1 pound fresh white cheese, shredded
1 egg
1 teaspoon baking powder

1 cup yuca flour
Salt to taste

Preheat the oven to 400 degrees. Combine the cheese and egg in a bowl and mix well. Add the baking powder and mix well. Add the yuca flour gradually, kneading until a soft dough forms. Add salt if necessary, depending on the saltiness of the cheese. Roll the dough into thirty small balls. Roll and shape each ball into a "U." Arrange 1 1/2 inches apart on greased baking sheets. Bake for 20 minutes.

Having trouble finding the right cheese? Try asking for queso blanco in the Latin section of your favorite supermarket. Pan de Yuca is great served with yogurt or butter, or with coffee in the morning.

Due to its large and elaborate canal system, Fort Lauderdale is known as the "Venice of America." Fort Lauderdale offers more than 300 miles of navigable intercoastal waterways stretching from the Atlantic Ocean to the Everglades.

zucchini chocolate nut bread

MAKES 2 LOAVES

3 eggs	1 teaspoon salt
2 cups sugar	1 tablespoon cinnamon
1 cup vegetable oil	$1/2$ teaspoon ground cloves
1 tablespoon vanilla extract	1 teaspoon nutmeg
2 cups grated zucchini	1 teaspoon baking powder
3 cups all-purpose flour	1 cup chopped walnuts
2 teaspoons baking soda	1 cup (6 ounces) chocolate chips

Preheat the oven to 350 degrees. Beat the eggs until light and foamy. Add the sugar, oil and vanilla and mix well. Stir in the zucchini. Add the flour, baking soda, salt, cinnamon, cloves, nutmeg and baking powder, stirring just until mixed. Stir in the walnuts and chocolate chips. Pour into two greased 5x9-inch loaf pans. Bake for 1 hour.

appetizers
& drinks
served

sponsor
PROVISIONAL CLASS 2007–2008

P.S.

Every fall, the Junior League of Greater Fort Lauderdale welcomes a new Provisional Class. Together with a team of Active Member Educators, these seventy women spend the year learning about our organization, visiting our legacy projects, and contributing to current projects and fund-raisers, like our cookbooks!

sausage and arugula grilled pizza

MAKES 4 TO 6 SERVINGS

1 garlic clove	Dough for one pizza crust
3/4 cup extra-virgin olive oil	10 to 16 ounces fontina cheese, shredded
1/2 red onion, thinly sliced	1 bunch basil leaves, chopped
8 ounces Italian sausage, casings removed	1 teaspoon pizza seasoning or Italian seasoning
8 ounces baby portobello mushrooms	16 ounces arugula

Combine the garlic and olive oil in a saucepan. Cook over medium heat for 1 to 2 minutes or until the garlic is golden brown.

Sauté the onion in a sauté pan for 5 minutes and then add the sausage. Cook until the sausage is brown and crumbly. Reduce the heat to low and add the mushrooms. Cook, covered, for 5 minutes. Roll out the dough on a lightly floured flat surface. Brush with some of the garlic oil. Place on the grill, oiled side down. Brush the other side with some of the garlic oil and grill, covered, for 1 minute. Layer the sausage mixture, cheese, basil and pizza seasoning evenly over the crust. Grill, covered, for 5 minutes. Remove from the grill and top with the arugula. Drizzle with the remaining garlic oil. Cut into slices to serve.

Photo, page 26: *Sunsetinis, recipe page 46; Tri This Hummus, recipe page 41; Sweet and Spicy Mango Salsa, recipe page 42*

caramelized onion and portobello mushroom pizza

Dough for one pizza crust

2 tablespoons extra-virgin olive oil

1 large Vidalia onion, sliced

Dash of salt

Dash of pepper

1 cup chopped portobello mushrooms or baby portobello mushrooms, sliced

1/2 cup cornmeal

2 tablespoons extra-virgin olive oil

1 1/2 cups tomato sauce

3 Roma tomatoes

1/2 cup feta cheese

2 cups (8 ounces) shredded mozzarella cheese

1 bunch fresh basil, shredded

Salt and pepper to taste

Preheat a pizza stone in a 410-degree oven. Let the dough rise for 10 minutes. Heat 2 tablespoons olive oil in a sauté pan and sauté the onion with the salt and pepper for 12 minutes, stirring occasionally. Add the mushrooms and cook for 8 minutes longer, stirring occasionally.

Roll out the dough on a surface sprinkled with the cornmeal. Arrange on the pizza stone. Drizzle with 2 tablespoons olive oil and bake for 10 minutes. Reduce the heat to 400 degrees. Combine the tomato sauce and tomatoes and spread over the pizza crust. Spread the onion and mushroom mixture evenly over the sauce. Sprinkle sparingly with the feta cheese. Top with the mozzarella cheese and basil and season with salt and pepper. Bake for 15 minutes longer. Let stand for 5 minutes before slicing.

Opened in the 1920s, Fort Lauderdale's Port Everglades is the deepest port in Florida, as well as the third busiest cruise port in the world. Port Everglades holds the world record for the most cruise passengers in a single day, with more than four million passengers traveling annually.

the best tailgating sandwiches

MAKES 36 SERVINGS

1/2 cup (1 stick) butter	1 tablespoon mustard
3 tablespoons poppy seeds	1 (36-count) pan small dinner rolls
1 teaspoon Worcestershire sauce	8 ounces ham, sliced
1 teaspoon minced fresh garlic	4 ounces Muenster cheese, sliced
8 ounces cream cheese, softened	4 ounces Cheddar cheese, sliced

Preheat the oven to 350 degrees. Melt the butter in a small saucepan or microwave-safe bowl. Add the poppy seeds, Worcestershire sauce and garlic and mix well. Combine the cream cheese and mustard in a small bowl and mix well. Slice the block of rolls into halves horizontally. Spread the cream cheese mixture thinly over the cut sides. Layer the ham, Muenster cheese and Cheddar cheese over the bottom half. Replace the top half and brush generously with the butter mixture. Bake for 10 minutes or until the cheeses melt.

bruschetta toasters

6 small to medium tomatoes, cut into halves, seeded and coarsely chopped
1/4 cup olive oil
5 garlic cloves, minced
2 tablespoons balsamic vinegar
3 tablespoons raw cane sugar

1/4 cup chopped fresh basil
1/2 teaspoon kosher salt
Freshly ground pepper to taste
1 loaf baguette
Olive oil
Kosher salt to taste

Combine the tomatoes, 1/4 cup olive oil, the garlic, vinegar, sugar, basil, 1/2 teaspoon salt and pepper. Let stand for at least 2 to 3 hours at room temperature or refrigerate for 8 to 12 hours. Cut the bread into slices. Coat each slice with olive oil and salt. Heat a grill pan over medium-high heat. Grill the bread slices on both sides until golden brown. Serve topped with the tomato mixture.

parmesan puffs

MAKES 8 SERVINGS

8 ounces cream cheese, softened
8 ounces Parmesan cheese, grated

2 eggs
Bread crumbs for coating

Combine the cream cheese, Parmesan cheese and eggs in a bowl and mix well. Chill, covered, in the refrigerator for 2 hours or longer. Preheat the oven to 350 degrees. Roll pieces of the cheese mixture into small balls the diameter of a half-dollar. Flatten slightly. Coat with bread crumbs. Arrange on an ungreased baking sheet. Bake for 15 minutes.

chilled asian spring rolls

3/4 cup finely shredded carrots
1/4 cup thinly sliced scallions
1 teaspoon rice vinegar, or to taste
Salt and pepper to taste
12 (6 1/2-inch-round) sheets rice paper
3/4 cup fresh cilantro leaves

1 pound shredded cooked chicken
3/4 cup finely shredded Bibb lettuce
3/4 cup alfalfa sprouts or bean sprouts
Cilantro sprigs for garnish
Cashew Dipping Sauce (below)

Combine the carrots, scallions, vinegar, salt and pepper in a small bowl and mix well. Fill a small cake pan or baking pan with water. Submerge four rice paper sheets in the water for 45 seconds to soften. Arrange the rice sheets in a single layer on paper towels to drain. Remove one rice sheet and cover the remaining rice sheets with a damp paper towel to prevent drying. Arrange 1 tablespoon of the cilantro in a horizontal line across the bottom of the rice sheet, leaving a 1-inch border all around. Top with 2 tablespoons of the chicken and 1 tablespoon of the carrot mixture. Sprinkle with 1 tablespoon of the lettuce and 1 tablespoon of the alfalfa sprouts. Season with salt and pepper. Roll to enclose the filling, tucking in the sides. Repeat with the remaining rice sheets and filling.

To serve, cut the rolls into halves diagonally with a serrated knife. Arrange the halves on a platter and garnish with cilantro. Serve with Cashew Dipping Sauce.

The spring rolls may be prepared up to 6 hours in advance. Arrange the rolls on a serving tray. Cover with paper towels and then with plastic wrap. Refrigerate until ready to serve.

cashew dipping sauce

1 cup (about 4 ounces) unsalted roasted cashews
1 tablespoon vegetable oil
3/4 cup plain yogurt
2 garlic cloves, minced

1 tablespoon fresh lemon juice, or to taste
1 tablespoon soy sauce, or to taste
Cayenne pepper to taste

Combine the cashews and oil in a blender or food processor. Process until the mixture forms a paste. Add the yogurt, garlic, lemon juice, soy sauce and cayenne pepper and mix until well blended. Chill, covered, in the refrigerator. Bring to room temperature before serving.

Chef Chris Wilber has been delighting diners since 1994 in his cozy and hip Fort Lauderdale eatery, Canyon Restaurant. This hot spot is where you can find his fun fusion of southwest and South Florida fare. As for his unique cooking style, Chef Wilber says, "I get crazy ideas, and I just try and go with them."

herb and goat cheese-stuffed poblano

MAKES 6 SERVINGS

6 (2- to 2 1/2-ounce) poblano chiles, stems on
8 ounces goat cheese, at room temperature
4 ounces cream cheese, softened
2 ounces (about 2/3 cup) freshly grated Parmesan cheese
1/2 cup lightly packed chopped cilantro
1/4 cup lightly packed chopped fresh basil

Salt and pepper to taste
2 eggs, lightly beaten
2/3 cup blue or yellow cornmeal
Peanut oil for frying
2 cups medium salsa, puréed
6 cilantro sprigs for garnish

Preheat the broiler. Broil the chiles on rack near heat or flame until the skin blisters all over, turning with tongs every 1 1/2 to 2 minutes. Cool on wire rack lined with paper towels. Remove the skins and cut a slit vertically in each chile. Remove the seeds and drain cut side down on the paper towels.

Process the goat cheese, cream cheese, Parmesan cheese, cilantro and basil in a blender or food processor until well combined. Season with salt and pepper. Fill each chile completely. Press the cut edges of the chiles together to enclose the filling. Dip each chile into the eggs and then roll in the cornmeal.

Heat 2 inches of peanut oil in a deep sauté pan over medium-high heat to about 350 degrees. Add the chiles. Cook for 5 minutes or until golden brown, turning frequently. Drain on paper towels.

Heat the salsa in a nonreactive saucepan over low heat. Spoon 1/3 cup of the salsa onto each of six warm serving plates. Top each with a stuffed chile and garnish with a cilantro sprig.

This recipe is from the kitchen of Chef Chris Wilber.

paradise served

armadillo eggs

16 ounces Cheddar cheese, cut into bite-size cubes
1 (32-ounce) jar seeded whole jalapeño chiles
1 pound mild or medium bulk turkey sausage

1 (10-count) can large refrigerator biscuits
Salsa

Preheat the oven according to the biscuit package directions. Place a cheese cube inside each jalapeño chile. Press enough sausage around each jalapeño chile to enclose completely. Separate the biscuits and roll each into a circle large enough to enclose one jalapeño chile. Wrap each jalapeño chile with a biscuit circle, pinching the edges to seal. Arrange on a baking sheet and bake for 20 to 30 minutes or until the sausage is cooked through. Serve with your favorite salsa.

florida firecrackers

24 jalapeño chiles
1 pound bulk pork sausage

16 ounces cream cheese, softened

Prepare the jalapeño chiles at least 4 to 24 hours before serving time. Cut the jalapeño chiles into halves lengthwise and remove the membranes and seeds, wearing latex gloves to prevent the chiles from burning the skin and eyes.

Preheat the oven to 350 degrees. Brown the sausage in a sauté pan until cooked through, stirring until crumbly; drain. Combine the sausage and cream cheese in a bowl and mix well. Stuff each jalapeño chile with the sausage mixture. Arrange on a baking sheet and bake for 25 to 30 minutes.

honey nut brie

1 (12-ounce) wedge Brie cheese   1/4 cup toasted sliced almonds
1/4 cup honey

Preheat the oven to 350 degrees. Place the cheese in a shallow baking dish. Drizzle with the honey and sprinkle with the almonds. Bake for 10 minutes. Serve with thick slices of baguette.

gorgonzola-stuffed dates

MAKES 12 SERVINGS

24 pitted dates   24 walnut halves, toasted
8 ounces creamy Gorgonzola cheese   1/4 cup walnut-flavored honey

Cut a slit in each date. Spoon a generous amount of cheese into each date. Press a walnut half into each date. Place on a serving platter. Drizzle with the honey.

P.S.

Chef Matthew Ludka cooks at the ultimate seaside spot, aboard the Gallant Lady, owned by the Moran family of JM Family Enterprises. Travel has inspired Chef Ludka's dishes for twenty-five years, as he seeks to fuse the different cuisines with local cultures. This recipe comes from his greatest inspiration, his wife, Ina, and her Jamaican heritage.

jerk chicken wings with mango green onion dip

MAKES 10 TO 12 SERVINGS

2 tablespoons wet (not dry) jerk seasoning
1/2 tablespoon olive oil
3 pounds chicken wings
1 mango, pitted and cut into halves
2 tablespoons orange juice

1 cup mayonnaise
3 green onions, thinly sliced
1 teaspoon grated fresh ginger
Sliced green onions for garnish
Chopped mango for garnish

Combine the jerk seasoning and olive oil in a bowl and mix well. Rub on the chicken wings. Marinate, covered, in the refrigerator for 2 to 12 hours.

Chop one-half of the mango. Purée the remaining mango half with the orange juice. Combine the mango purée with the mayonnaise, green onions, ginger and chopped mango in a bowl and mix well.

Grill the chicken wings over medium-high heat for 20 minutes or until the skin is crisp and the juices run clear when pierced with a knife, or bake at 425 degrees for 20 to 25 minutes. Serve with the mango dipping sauce and garnish with green onions and mango.

This recipe is from the kitchen of Chef Matthew Ludka.

easy swedish meatballs

Meatballs	**Mushroom Sauce**
1/2 cup finely chopped onion	8 ounces fresh mushrooms, sliced
2 tablespoons butter	3 tablespoons butter
1 cup soft bread crumbs	1 tablespoon flour
2/3 cup milk	3/4 cup half-and-half
2 eggs, beaten	Salt and pepper to taste
2 teaspoons salt	1 or 2 pinches of garlic powder
1/2 teaspoon allspice	1 teaspoon soy sauce
1/4 teaspoon pepper	Red wine (optional)
2 pounds ground beef	

For the meatballs, preheat the oven to 350 degrees. Sauté the onion in the butter in a skillet until tender. Soak the bread crumbs in the milk in a bowl for 5 minutes. Add the eggs, salt, allspice and pepper and mix well. Stir in the onion mixture and ground beef. Shape into balls, using a slightly rounded tablespoon of ground beef mixture for each. Arrange in a greased shallow baking pan. Bake for 18 to 20 minutes or until cooked through. Remove the meatballs to a serving dish.

For the mushroom sauce, sauté the mushrooms in the butter in a skillet until tender. Stir in the flour until blended. Add the half-and-half gradually, stirring constanly. Add salt, pepper, garlic powder and soy sauce and cook until thickened and smooth, stirring constantly. Thin with a small amount of red wine if the sauce is too thick. Pour over the meatballs to serve.

If you prefer to make the meatballs in advance, chill, covered, until ready to cook.

tropical mango slide

Clams

24 Cedar Key clams or hard-shell clams

Water

White wine to taste

Minced garlic to taste

Ice water

Pinch of kosher salt

Mango Salsa

2 ripe mangoes, chopped

1 1/2 tablespoons minced seeded jalapeño chile, or to taste

1/4 cup coarsely chopped cilantro

2 tablespoons fresh lime juice, or to taste

1/2 teaspoon kosher salt

1/4 cup chopped red onion, or to taste

Lime juice for garnish

Chopped jalapeño chile for garnish

Assembly

Crushed ice

Rock salt

For the clams, steam the clams in a mixture of water, white wine and garlic. Cool and then separate the clams from the shells. Place the clams in a bowl. Reserve half of the shells. Place the reserved shells in ice water in a bowl. Add a pinch of kosher salt.

For the mango salsa, combine the mangoes, jalapeño chile, cilantro, lime juice, 1/2 teaspoon salt and the onion in a bowl and toss to combine.

To assemble, place a clam on each shell half. Top with a small amount of the mango salsa. Garnish with extra lime juice and jalapeño chile. Pack a serving tray with ice. Sprinkle with rock salt to prevent the ice from melting. Arrange the clams on the ice. Serve immediately or refrigerate for up to 1 hour.

No fork required—just tip the clam shell and let the Tropical Mango Slide . . . Bon appétit!

fancy baked oysters

MAKES 8 TO 10 SERVINGS

24 small oysters in shells
3/4 cup bread crumbs
1/4 cup chopped fresh parsley
2 garlic cloves, minced
2 tablespoons minced shallots

1/2 cup (1 stick) butter
2 tablespoons fresh lemon juice
Salt and pepper to taste
1/4 cup crumbled crisp-cooked bacon

Open the oysters, discarding the top shell. Arrange the oysters on a baking sheet. Preheat the oven to 375 degrees. Combine the bread crumbs and parsley in a bowl and mix well. Sauté the garlic and shallots in the butter in a small sauté pan for 1 minute. Stir in the lemon juice, salt and pepper.

Top each oyster with 1 tablespoon of the bread crumb mixture. Drizzle each with the garlic butter mixture. Top each with some bacon. Bake for 20 minutes. Serve warm.

You may prepare the oysters for baking and chill, covered, until baking time.

P.S.

To keep tropical fruits such as mangoes, pineapples, Key limes, star fruit and passion fruit fresh longer, store them on your countertop at room temperature—never in your refrigerator.

mango and shrimp ceviche

MAKES 10 TO 12 SERVINGS

2 green or ripe mangoes or one of each, chopped
1/2 cup chopped red onion
1 or 2 jalapeño chiles, chopped
Juice of 2 limes

1 garlic clove, finely chopped
1/2 teaspoon salt
3 tablespoons cilantro, or to taste
1 pound peeled cooked shrimp, cut into 1/2-inch pieces

Combine the mangoes, onion, jalapeño chiles, lime juice, garlic, salt, cilantro and shrimp in a large bowl and mix well. Let stand for 30 minutes or longer to allow the flavors to blend.

tri this hummus

1 (16-ounce) can chick-peas,
rinsed and drained
1/2 cup tahini

Juice of 1 lemon
Salt and pepper to taste
1/3 cup olive oil

Combine the chick-peas, tahini, lemon juice, garlic, salt and pepper in a food processor fitted with a metal blade. Process until blended. Add the olive oil gradually, processing constantly until of the desired texture. You may not need to use all of the olive oil. Chill for about 1 hour.

To make Black Bean Hummus, substitute one 15-ounce can black beans for the chick-peas. To make Edamame Hummus, substitute 8 ounces shelled edamame for the chick-peas. You may also prepare all three variations and serve this trio together. Serve with pita pieces, bagel chips or crackers.

black bean and corn salsa

MAKES 10 TO 12 SERVINGS

1 (15-ounce) can yellow whole kernel corn,
rinsed and drained
2 (15-ounce) cans black beans, rinsed
and drained
1 tablespoon minced garlic
1/4 cup chopped red or purple onion
1/3 cup chopped fresh cilantro

1 (15-ounce) can spicy chopped tomatoes
Juice of 1 lime
2 tablespoons olive oil
2 tablespoons cumin
Salt and pepper to taste
Lime wedge for garnish

Combine the corn and beans in a large bowl and mix well. Add the garlic, onion, cilantro and tomatoes and mix well. Add the lime juice and olive oil. Sprinkle with cumin, salt and pepper and mix well. The salsa is good served with tortilla chips and over grilled chicken breasts. Chill for 1 to 2 hours before serving.

For easy mixing, prepare the salsa in a large plastic container with a tight-fitting lid and shake to blend. You may also purée the salsa and use in Mexican dishes.

texas caviar

1 (15-ounce) can white whole kernel corn, rinsed and drained

1 (15-ounce) can black-eyed peas, rinsed and drained

1 (4-ounce) can green chilies

1 (10-ounce) can tomatoes with green chiles

Cumin to taste

1/2 cup Italian salad dressing

Combine the corn, black-eyed peas, chiles, tomatoes with chiles, cumin and salad dressing in a large bowl and mix well. Serve with tortilla chips.

sweet and spicy mango salsa

2 ripe mangoes, cut into cubes

1 small red onion, chopped

1 large tomato, chopped

1 garlic clove, minced or pressed

1 bunch fresh cilantro, chopped

Juice of 1 lime

1 teaspoon Sweet & Spicy Tabasco sauce

Combine the mangoes, onion, tomato, garlic and cilantro in a serving bowl and mix well. Add the lime juice and Tabasco sauce and mix well. Serve with tortilla chips.

The salsa also makes an excellent garnish for grilled chicken, pork, or fish.

strawberry salsa

1 pint strawberries, chopped

4 plum tomatoes, seeded and chopped

1 small red onion, chopped

1 or 2 jalapeño chiles, minced

Juice of 1 lime

2 garlic cloves, minced

1 tablespoon olive oil

Combine the strawberries, tomatoes, onion and jalapeño chiles in a bowl and mix well. Stir in the lime juice, garlic and olive oil. Chill, covered, for 2 hours. Serve with chicken, pork or tortilla chips.

fiery fiesta spread

MAKES 4 SERVINGS

8 ounces regular or light cream cheese, softened

1/2 cup salsa

1/2 cup apricot preserves or orange marmalade

1 tablespoon chopped fresh cilantro

1 bunch green onions, thinly sliced

1/2 green bell pepper, chopped

1/4 cup (1 ounce) shredded Cheddar cheese

1 to 2 tablespoons chopped black olives

1 small avocado, chopped

1 to 2 tablespoons chopped jalapeño chiles (optional)

Place the cream cheese on a serving plate and flatten to about a 1/2-inch thickness. Combine the salsa and preserves in a bowl and mix well. Spread over the cream cheese. Sprinkle with the cilantro, green onions, bell pepper, cheese, olives, avocado and jalapeño chiles. Serve with assorted crackers.

spicy crab and artichoke dip

16 ounces cream cheese, softened
1 (6-ounce) jar marinated artichoke hearts, drained and chopped
2 (6-ounce) cans fancy white crab meat
3 tablespoons minced green onions

2 tablespoons prepared horseradish
2 teaspoons Worcestershire sauce
2 tablespoons Tabasco sauce
Dash of paprika

Preheat the oven to 375 degrees. Beat the cream cheese with a mixer or in a food processor until smooth. Add the artichoke hearts, crab meat, green onions, horseradish, Worcestershire sauce and Tabasco sauce and mix well. Spread the cream cheese mixture in a 9-inch baking dish. Sprinkle with paprika. Bake for 25 minutes or until heated through. Serve with crackers, bread or vegetable crudités.

savory pecan spread

8 ounces cream cheese, softened
2 tablespoons milk
2 ounces dried beef, chopped
1/4 cup chopped green bell pepper
2 tablespoons minced onion
1/2 cup sour cream

1/2 teaspoon minced garlic
1/4 teaspoon pepper
1 to 2 tablespoons chopped pickled jalapeño chile
2 tablespoons butter
1/2 cup chopped pecans

Preheat the oven to 350 degrees. Beat the cream cheese and the milk with an electric mixer. Stir in the beef, bell pepper, onion, sour cream, garlic, pepper and jalapeño chile and mix well. Pour into a 1-quart baking dish.

Melt the butter in a small sauté pan and add the pecans. Sauté over medium-high heat until light brown. Spread the pecans over the cream cheese mixture. Bake for 20 minutes.

A great way to serve this recipe is with wheat crackers or warm over baked potatoes.

salmon ball

2 cups canned salmon, drained, flaked
and bones removed

8 ounces reduced-fat cream cheese, softened

1 tablespoon finely chopped onion

1 tablespoon lemon juice

1 teaspoon prepared horseradish

1/4 teaspoon salt

1/4 teaspoon liquid smoke (optional)

1/2 cup chopped pecans or almonds

2 tablespoons parsley

Combine the salmon, cream cheese, onion, lemon juice, horseradish, salt and liquid smoke in a large bowl and mix well. (Use an electric mixer, if desired.) Chill in the refrigerator for 4 hours or until mixture is firm enough to hold a shape.

Combine the pecans and parsley in a small bowl. Shape the salmon mixture into a ball. Roll the salmon ball in the pecan mixture to coat. Chill in the refrigerator for 1 hour or longer. Serve with carrot chips or crackers.

seven-layer shrimp spread

1 pound cooked shrimp

8 ounces cream cheese, softened

1/4 cup lemon juice

1 tablespoon mayonnaise

1 teaspoon Old Bay seasoning

1/4 teaspoon Worcestershire sauce

Dash of Tabasco sauce

1 (12-ounce) jar cocktail sauce

2 cups (8 ounces) shredded Monterey
Jack cheese

3 green onions, sliced

1/2 cup chopped green bell pepper

1/4 cup black olives, sliced

Parsley or watercress for garnish

Chop half of the shrimp. Chill all of the shrimp in the refrigerator. Beat the cream cheese with the lemon juice, mayonnaise, Old Bay seasoning, Worcestershire sauce and Tabasco sauce until smooth. Spread the mixture in a serving dish. Chill in the refrigerator for 30 minutes or longer. Spread the cocktail sauce over the cream cheese mixture. Top with the chopped shrimp, cheese, green onions, bell pepper and olives. Top with the whole shrimp. Garnish with parsley. Serve with crackers.

cream soda martinis

8 shots vanilla vodka
2 shots Triple Sec

2 shots ginger ale
2 to 4 maraschino cherries

Combine the vodka, Triple Sec and ginger ale with the ice in a cocktail shaker. Cover and shake well. Pour into martini glasses and garnish each with a cherry.

sunsetinis

2 shots orange vodka
1 shot Triple Sec
4 shots cranberry juice

2 teaspoons fresh lime juice
Orange zest, cut into long strips

Combine the orange vodka, Triple Sec, cranberry juice and lime juice with ice in a cocktail shaker. Cover and shake well. Strain into two large martini glasses. Garnish with strips of orange zest.

mocha espresso martinis

MAKES 2 SERVINGS

1 shot vanilla vodka	1/2 shot chocolate liqueur
1 shot coffee liqueur	Ice
2 shots coffee cream liqueur	6 coffee beans

Combine the vodka, coffee liqueur, coffee cream liqueur, chocolate liqueur and ice in a cocktail shaker. Cover and shake well. Strain into two large chilled martini glasses. Garnish each with 3 coffee beans.

low key 1-2-3s

MAKES 12 SERVINGS

1 cup pure maple syrup	3 cups vodka
2 cups fresh lemon juice	

Combine the maple syrup, lemon juice and vodka in a pitcher and mix well. Serve over ice.

grapefruit daiquiris

MAKES 2 SERVINGS

Juice of 1 pink grapefruit
2 shots dark rum
Splash of Cointreau or Grand Marnier

1/2 teaspoon superfine sugar
Juice of 1/2 lime
10 to 12 ice cubes

Combine the grapefruit juice, rum, Cointreau, sugar, lime juice and ice in a blender. Process until frothy.

open house punch

25 ounces Southern Comfort
16 ounces cranberry juice cocktail
8 ounces fresh lemon juice

Dash of Angostura bitters
32 ounces lemon-lime soda, very cold

Combine the Southern Comfort, cranberry juice cocktail, lemon juice and bitters in a punch bowl and mix well. Add the soda just before serving. To replenish the punch, add additional soda, cranberry juice cocktail and ice cubes.

paradise party punch

5 oranges
3 lemons
1 (46-ounce) can unsweetened
pineapple juice

1/2 cup sugar, or to taste
Block of ice
1 quart ginger ale
3 cups white rum

About 1 hour before serving time, juice four of the oranges and two of the lemons. Combine the juices with the pineapple juice in a pitcher. Add the sugar and mix well. Cut the remaining orange and lemon into thin slices and then cut into triangles. Add to the pitcher and mix well. Let stand, covered, until serving time. Place the ice into a punch bowl. Add the ginger ale and rum to the juice mixture. Pour over the ice.

suntan lotion

MAKES 1 SERVING

1 generous shot coconut rum   2 lime wedges
8 ounces club soda

Mix the rum and club soda and pour over ice in a glass. Squeeze one lime wedge into the drink. Use the remaining lime wedge to garnish the drink.

mango smoothie

3 mangoes

8 ounces vanilla yogurt

1 banana

2 cups fresh orange juice

Juice of 1 lime

1 cup crushed ice

Pinch of salt

2 tablespoons protein powder (optional)

Combine the mangoes, yogurt, banana, orange juice, lime juice, ice, salt and protein powder in a blender. Process on high for at least 3 minutes or until very smooth.

strawbana smoothie

MAKES 2 SERVINGS

10 ounces frozen whole strawberries

1 banana

1 cup vanilla frozen yogurt

1/2 cup ice

1 cup strawberry kiwi juice

Whipped cream to taste

Strawberry syrup to taste

Combine the strawberries, banana, frozen yogurt, ice and juice in a blender. Process on high until smooth. Pour into two glasses. Top with whipped cream. Drizzle with strawberry syrup.

soups
& salads
served

tuscan bean vegetable soup

MAKES 12 TO 15 SERVINGS

2 tablespoons olive oil

1 small yellow onion, chopped

1 pound chopped ham (optional)

16 ounces navy beans, soaked and drained

8 cups chicken broth

2 small to medium zucchini

2 small to medium yellow squash

3 carrots

1/2 each red and yellow bell pepper

1 (8 ounce) can chopped tomatoes

1 teaspoon each salt, pepper and garlic powder

1 teaspoon Worcestershire sauce

1 teaspoon Tabasco sauce

1 teaspoon each basil and thyme

8 ounces Parmesan cheese, grated

Heat the olive oil in a stockpot. Add the onion and ham and sauté until the onion is golden brown. Add the remaining ingredients, except the cheese. Simmer, covered, over medium-low heat for 4 hours, stirring occasionally. Ladle into bowls. Sprinkle with the cheese.

egyptian bean soup

MAKES 4 TO 6 SERVINGS

1 cup chopped onion

2 garlic cloves, minced

1/4 cup olive oil

1 teaspoon ground cumin

1 1/2 teaspoons sweet Hungarian paprika

1/4 teaspoon cayenne pepper

2 bay leaves

1 large carrot, chopped

1 cup chopped fresh tomatoes

4 cups vegetable stock

2 cups canned fava beans

1/4 cup chopped fresh parsley

3 tablespoons fresh lemon juice

Salt and pepper to taste

Mint leaves for garnish

Sauté the onion and garlic in the olive oil in a stockpot until the onion is translucent. Add the cumin, paprika, cayenne pepper, bay leaves and carrot and cook over medium heat for 5 minutes. Stir in the tomatoes and stock. Simmer for about 15 minutes or until the carrots are tender. Add the beans, parsley, lemon juice, salt and pepper and heat through. Garnish with mint leaves.

Photo, page 52: *Hearts of Palm Salad, recipe page 67*

P.S.

Incorporated in 1911, Fort Lauderdale is a major tourist destination with more than 23 miles of sandy beaches bordering the Atlantic Ocean and more than 2,500 award~winning restaurants. During the 1970s, Fort Lauderdale was known as a popular college spring break destination. Today we attract sun~loving tourists from all over the world.

split pea and barley soup

MAKES 10 SERVINGS

3 (6-ounce) bags Manischewitz split pea
and barley soup mix
1 (16-ounce) bag split peas
1 (8-ounce) bag dried baby lima beans

2 carrots, chopped
1 gallon water
Salt and pepper to taste

Combine the soup mix, peas, lima beans, carrots, water, salt and pepper in a stockpot. Bring to a boil over high heat. Reduce the heat to simmer. Cook for 3 hours, stirring occasionally and scraping the bottom to prevent sticking. Blend with an immersion blender until smooth. (Or process in a blender in batches until smooth.) Soup will be thick; add water or chicken broth until the soup is of the desired consistency.

cream of broccoli soup

1 1/2 pounds fresh broccoli, cut into small pieces

3 cups chicken broth

9 tablespoons (1 stick plus 1 tablespoon) butter, melted

6 tablespoons (heaping) all-purpose flour

Salt and pepper to taste

3/8 teaspoon nutmeg (optional)

6 cups half-and-half

Shredded Cheddar cheese for garnish

Cook the broccoli in the broth in a stockpot until tender. Drain, reserving the broth. Set the broccoli aside. Combine the butter and flour in the stockpot. Add the reserved broth and whisk until smooth. Heat until mixture is hot. Add the broccoli, salt, pepper, nutmeg and half-and-half. Garnish with cheese.

The soup can be prepared in advance and frozen.

white corn chowder

3 tablespoons butter

2 garlic cloves, minced

4 shallots, chopped

1/2 jalapeño chile, roasted, seeded and chopped

1 cup chicken broth

3 cups white fresh or frozen corn kernels

1 1/2 cups cream

Salt to taste

Chopped cilantro

Melt the butter in a saucepan. Add the garlic and shallots and sauté until tender. Add the jalapeño chile and sauté briefly. Add the broth, corn and cream and mix well. Bring to a boil. Reduce the heat to low and simmer for 5 minutes. Purée the mixture in a blender. Return the soup to the saucepan. Season with salt. Reheat until hot; do not boil. Garnish with cilantro.

southwest chili

2 pounds lean ground beef
1 cup chopped onion
1 envelope taco seasoning mix
1 (15-ounce) can pinto beans, rinsed and drained
1 (15-ounce) can black beans, rinsed and drained
1 (15-ounce) can spicy stewed tomatoes

1 (15-ounce) can diced tomatoes
1 (10-ounce) can tomatoes with green chiles
1 (4-ounce) can chopped green chilies
1/4 cup chopped cilantro
Sour cream
Cheddar cheese
Cilantro sprigs

Sauté the beef with the onion and taco seasoning mix in a sauté pan, stirring until brown and crumbly; drain. Combine the beef mixture with the beans, tomatoes, chiles and cilantro in a slow cooker. Cook on low for 6 hours. Top with sour cream, cheese and cilantro.

vegetarian chili

1 tablespoon canola oil
1 onion, chopped
1 (28-ounce) can chopped tomatoes
1 cup sliced carrots
1 cup sliced celery
1 red bell pepper, chopped
1/2 cup water

1 teaspoon ground cumin
1/8 teaspoon red pepper flakes (optional)
1 (16-ounce) can light red kidney beans or pinto beans
2 cups cooked brown rice
Salt and pepper to taste

Heat the canola oil in a large saucepan over medium heat. Add the onion and sauté for 6 minutes or until tender, stirring constantly. Add the tomatoes, carrots, celery, bell pepper, water, cumin and pepper flakes and mix well. Simmer, covered, for 30 minutes, stirring occasionally. Stir in the beans and rice. Cook for 5 minutes longer or until heated through. Season with salt and pepper.

tortellini soup

1 tablespoon butter
4 to 6 garlic cloves, pressed or minced
32 ounces chicken broth or vegetable broth
1 (9-ounce) package fresh three-cheese tortellini
Salt and freshly ground pepper to taste

1 (14-ounce) can chopped stewed tomatoes
1/2 (8-ounce) bag fresh spinach, stems removed
1/2 cup loosely packed chopped fresh basil
Freshly shaved or grated Parmesan cheese

Melt the butter in a saucepan over medium-low heat, taking care not to burn the butter. Add the garlic and sauté for 3 to 4 minutes or until tender but not brown. Add the broth and tortellini. Bring to a boil over medium-high heat. Simmer for 8 to 10 minutes or until the tortellini are tender. Season with salt and pepper. Add the tomatoes, spinach and basil and simmer for 8 to 10 minutes or until the spinach and basil are tender. Garnish with cheese.

kielbasa stew

2 tablespoons olive oil or vegetable oil
1 1/4 to 1 1/2 pounds fresh kielbasa or Italian
  sausage, chopped or casings removed
3 cups chopped potatoes
2 (14-ounce) cans tomatoes, undrained
2 (14-ounce) cans green beans, undrained
1 (15-ounce) can whole kernel corn, undrained

1 (8-ounce) can mushroom stems and
  pieces, undrained
2 garlic cloves, minced, or garlic powder to taste
1/4 cup chopped onion
2 (11-ounce) cans tomato juice or
  V-8 vegetable juice
Salt and pepper to taste

Heat the olive oil in a Dutch oven and sauté the kielbasa until brown and crumbly. Add the potatoes, tomatoes, beans, corn, mushrooms, garlic, onion, tomato juice, salt and pepper. Add enough water to fill the Dutch oven. Simmer at least until the potatoes are tender.

potato leek soup

2 to 4 tablespoons butter
1 cup chopped celery
1 cup sliced leeks, white and light green parts only
6 to 8 Idaho or Yukon Gold potatoes, peeled and cut into quarters

1 (12-ounce) can evaporated milk
Salt and pepper to taste
Bacon bits
Shredded cheese
Sliced scallions

Melt the butter in a sauté pan and sauté the celery and leeks until tender. Bring the potatoes and water to cover to boil in a stockpot. Simmer, covered, until fork tender. Reduce the heat. Use a potato masher to mash the potatoes into medium chunks. Remove 1 to 1 1/2 cups potato water and reserve. Add the evaporated milk to the potato mixture. Add the leeks and celery and mix well. For a thinner consistency, add the reserved potato water. Season with salt and pepper. Simmer until heated through. Garnish with bacon bits, cheese and scallions.

The soup thickens over time, so keep the reserved liquid to thin it, if needed. Water may be used, but potato liquid has more flavor.

curried pumpkin soup

1/4 cup butter
1 cup chopped onion
1 garlic clove, crushed
3 cups chicken broth
2 teaspoons curry powder
1 teaspoon ground coriander

1/2 teaspoon salt
1/4 teaspoon red pepper flakes
1 3/4 cups cooked pumpkin, or
    1 (16-ounce) can pumpkin purée
1 cup light cream (coffee cream)

Melt the butter in a large saucepan. Add the onion and garlic and sauté. Stir in the broth, curry powder, coriander, salt and pepper flakes. Simmer for 20 minutes. Stir in the pumpkin and cream. Simmer for 5 minutes.

You may prepare this soup in advance and refrigerate until serving time.

coconut shrimp soup

2 tablespoons olive oil
1/2 cup finely chopped onion
1/4 cup finely chopped red bell pepper
1/4 cup finely chopped green bell pepper
3 garlic cloves, finely chopped

3 to 4 teaspoons curry powder
1/4 teaspoon red pepper flakes
2 (14-ounce) cans chicken broth
1 (13-ounce) can coconut milk
1 pound uncooked shelled deveined shrimp

Heat the olive oil in a large saucepan. Add the onion, bell peppers and garlic and sauté until tender. Add the curry powder, pepper flakes, broth and coconut milk and bring to a boil. Add the shrimp. Cook for 5 minutes or until the shrimp turn pink. Purée the mixture in a blender or food processor. Serve hot.

gulf stream gazpacho

MAKES 4 SERVINGS

3 garlic cloves	3 ice cubes
3 tablespoons red wine vinegar	3 slices dry bread, cut into cubes
3 tablespoons olive oil	1 cup chopped green bell pepper
3 cups V-8 vegetable juice	2 cups chopped tomato
1/2 teaspoon Tabasco sauce	2/3 cup chopped onion
Dash of black pepper	1 1/2 cups chopped cucumber
1 cup cold water	1 cup garlic butter croutons

Combine the garlic, vinegar, olive oil and vegetable juice in a blender. Process until well blended. Add the Tabasco sauce, pepper, water and ice cubes. Process until well blended. Pour the vegetable juice mixture over the bread and vegetables in a bowl. Chill in the refrigerator for 30 minutes or longer. Top with croutons.

This recipe is from The Honorable Judge Jose A. Gonzales, Jr.

paradise served

sweet apple salad

1 egg, beaten
1 cup sugar
1/4 cup water
1/4 cup red wine vinegar
1 teaspoon yellow mustard
4 apples, peeled and chopped

16 ounces Cheddar cheese, chopped
1 (4-ounce) jar chopped pimentos, drained
1 1/2 tablespoons Tabasco sauce
1 tablespoon sugar
Lettuce leaves

Combine the egg, 1 cup sugar, the water, vinegar and mustard in a small saucepan. Cook over low heat until thickened and blended, stirring constantly. Let cool completely.

Combine the apple, cheese, pimentos, Tabasco sauce and 1 tablespoon sugar in a serving bowl. Toss gently to combine. Pour the dressing over the apple mixture and mix gently. Serve on lettuce leaves.

barley salad

1 cup barley, cooked
1/2 cup thinly sliced green onions
1 to 2 jalapeño chiles, minced
3 tablespoons vinegar
1/3 cup olive oil
2 cups cooked corn

1 large tomato, chopped
2 to 4 garlic cloves, minced
1/4 cup chopped cilantro
1/2 teaspoon cumin
1 (15-ounce) can black beans (optional)

Combine the barley, green onions, jalapeño chiles, vinegar, olive oil, corn, tomato, garlic, cilantro, cumin and beans in a large bowl and mix well. Chill in the refrigerator. Serve cold or at room temperature.

confetti broccoli salad

2 bunches broccoli, cut into florets
12 slices bacon, crisp-cooked and cut into
bite-size pieces
1/2 red onion, cut into 1/4- to 1/2-inch pieces
1/4 cup raisins

1/4 cup dried cranberries
1/4 cup dried blueberries
1 cup mayonnaise
1/2 cup sugar
2 tablespoons vinegar

Combine the broccoli, bacon, onion, raisins, cranberries and blueberries in a serving bowl. Combine the mayonnaise, sugar and vinegar in a small bowl and mix well. Add to the broccoli mixture and stir to coat. Chill in the refrigerator for 3 hours or longer, stirring occasionally.

asian chicken salad

2 (3-ounce) packages ramen noodles, crushed
4 cups chopped cooked chicken
1 cup shredded cabbage
1 (10-ounce) package baby spinach
3 ounces toasted sliced almonds
2 cups seedless red grapes
8 scallions, sliced

1 cup olive oil
6 tablespoons red wine vinegar or
balsamic vinegar
1/2 cup sugar, or 12 packets sugar substitute
3 tablespoons soy sauce
Dash of Worcestershire sauce

Discard the seasoning packets from the noodles. Combine the noodles, chicken, cabbage, spinach, almonds and grapes in a large bowl and toss to combine. Combine the scallions, olive oil, vinegar, sugar, soy sauce and Worcestershire sauce in a bowl and mix well. Pour over the salad and toss to coat.

fruited rosemary chicken salad

1 pound boneless skinless chicken breasts
1 sprig of rosemary
1 teaspoon kosher salt
1 teaspoon freshly cracked pepper
2 ribs celery, chopped
2 green onions, tops thinly sliced

1/2 cup red grape halves
3 tablespoons sliced almonds
1/3 cup low-fat plain yogurt
2 tablespoons mayonnaise
1 sprig of rosemary
Salt and pepper to taste

Combine the chicken with water to cover in a saucepan. Bring to a boil. Add 1 sprig of rosemary, 1 teaspoon salt and the 1 teaspoon pepper. Reduce the heat to medium-high and boil the chicken for 40 minutes. Remove the chicken from the water and let cool. Cut into 1/2-inch pieces. Combine with the celery, green onions, grapes and almonds. Stir in the yogurt, mayonnaise and the leaves from 1 sprig of rosemary; mix well. Season with salt and pepper to taste. Chill in the refrigerator for 8 hours or longer for the best flavor.

For a different flavor, substitute chopped apple, dried apricots or raisins for the grapes.

Orange you glad for oranges? Florida ranks #1 in citrus production, providing seventy percent of the U.S. crop every year. About ninety percent of these crops are used to make orange juice—the official beverage of Florida. Eat a whole orange and you'll get 130 percent of the recommended dietary allowance for Vitamin C!

citrus grove salad

MAKES 6 SERVINGS

2 red grapefruit	1/2 cup red grapefruit juice
4 navel oranges	2 teaspoons Dijon mustard
1 1/2 (5-ounce) bags mixed greens or Boston	2 teaspoons honey
lettuce and radicchio	2 teaspoons lemon juice
1/2 red onion, sliced thin	1 teaspoon salt
3/4 cup olive oil	1/4 teaspoon white pepper

Peel the grapefruit and oranges. Remove all the white pith. Cut the fruit into bite-size pieces. Tear the lettuce. Combine the lettuce, fruit and onion in a large salad bowl. Whisk the olive oil, grapefruit juice, Dijon mustard, honey, lemon juice, salt and pepper in a small bowl. Toss the salad with the dressing a few minutes before serving to allow flavors to blend.

blt pasta salad

Salad

6 cups drained cooked bow tie pasta

1 tablespoon olive oil

8 ounces bacon, chopped and crisp-cooked

2 cups cherry tomatoes or grape tomatoes,
cut into halves

1/2 cup chopped red onion (optional)

6 cups assorted mixed spring greens, or lettuce
of your choice

Creamy Parmesan Dressing

1/2 cup mayonnaise

1/2 cup (2 ounces) freshly grated
Parmesan cheese

1 tablespoon white wine vinegar

Freshly ground pepper to taste

For the salad, combine the pasta and olive oil in a serving bowl and toss to coat. Add the bacon, tomatoes, onion and lettuce.

For the dressing, combine the mayonnaise, Parmesan cheese and vinegar in a bowl and mix well. Pour over the salad and mix gently. Season with pepper.

easy antipasto salad

MAKES 6 TO 8 SERVINGS

16 ounces bow tie or penne pasta, cooked
and drained

16 ounces balsamic vinaigrette

1 (6- to 8-ounce) jar Spanish or Italian olives
(optional)

2 (6-ounce) cans pitted black olives

8 ounces Genoa salami, thinly sliced

8 ounces pepperoni, thinly sliced

2 (6-ounce) jars marinated artichoke hearts

2 cups (8 ounces) shredded mozzarella cheese

Combine the pasta in a large bowl with a small amount of the vinaigrette. Let cool. Drain the Spanish olives and black olives and add to the pasta. Chop the salami and pepperoni finely and add to the pasta. Drain and reserve the liquid from the artichoke hearts. Chop the artichoke hearts coarsely and add to the pasta along with the liquid and enough of the remaining vinaigrette to moisten the salad. Sprinkle with the cheese and toss to combine. Chill in the refrigerator for 30 minutes. Toss again just before serving.

Substitute any meat of your choice; roast beef and ham also make delicious choices.

Hearts of palm are literally the heart of the sabal palmetto. As our state tree, this graceful palm was once known as "swamp cabbage," since it was readily available to residents and was an important food source during the Depression. Once the delicate taste and tender flesh were widely discovered, the nickname quickly changed to "Millionaire's Salad."

hearts of palm salad

MAKES 6 SERVINGS

1 (14-ounce) can hearts of palm, drained and sliced

1 (14-ounce) can artichoke hearts, drained and cut into quarters

1/2 cup chopped green bell pepper

1/2 cup chopped red bell pepper

10 pimento-stuffed olives, cut into halves

10 pitted black olives

3 tablespoons olive oil

3 tablespoons vegetable oil

3 tablespoons wine vinegar

1/2 teaspoon Dijon mustard

1/2 teaspoon salt

1/2 teaspoon pepper

Combine the hearts of palm, artichoke hearts, bell peppers and olives in a large bowl. Combine the olive oil, vegetable oil, vinegar, Dijon mustard, salt and pepper in a bowl or a jar with a tight-fitting lid and mix well. Pour over the vegetables. Marinate for 1 hour before serving.

P.S.

Go green! Florida is one of four U.S. states that grows avocados. The Florida avocado, also known as the alligator pear, is named for its bright green color and creamy, nutty flavor. Most of Florida's avocados are grown in Miami–Dade County.

ceviche salad

MAKES 4 SERVINGS

1 cup fresh lime juice	1 pound sashimi-grade boneless skinless salmon, or shelled fresh shrimp
2 garlic cloves	
1 cup loosely packed coarsely chopped fresh cilantro	1 avocado, chopped
	1 large head Boston lettuce, torn
2 serrano chiles	1 scallion, chopped
1/2 teaspoon salt	

Combine the lime juice, garlic, cilantro, serrano chiles and salt in a blender or food processor. Process until smooth. Combine the salmon and the lime marinade in a large bowl. Chill in the refrigerator for a few minutes if you prefer sashimi-style ceviche, or let the mixture chill and "cook" in the refrigerator for 1 to 2 hours.

Drain half of the marinade and reserve. Add the avocado to the ceviche and toss to mix. Divide the lettuce among four serving plates. Spoon ceviche into the center of each plate. Sprinkle with the scallion. Drizzle with the reserved marinade.

warm potato salad niçoise

Shallot Vinaigrette

2 shallots, finely chopped

3 tablespoons white wine vinegar

2 tablespoons whole grain mustard

Salt and pepper to taste

1/2 cup extra-virgin olive oil

Salad

16 ounces small red or white potatoes

Salt to taste

6 ounces thin green beans

Olive oil

8 ounces grape tomatoes

6 ounces Italian tuna in oil

4 anchovy fillets, chopped

2 tablespoons drained capers

1/4 cup black olives, pitted and cut into halves (optional)

1 large bunch basil

For the shallot vinaigrette, combine the shallots, vinegar, mustard, salt and pepper in a jar with a tight-fitting lid. Shake to mix. Add the olive oil and shake again.

For the salad, simmer the potatoes in boiling salted water to cover for 15 minutes; drain. Let cool slightly. Cut into halves. Combine with the dressing in a salad bowl.

Cook the green beans in boiling salted water for 2 minutes; drain. Add to the potatoes and toss to coat.

Preheat the oven to 400 degrees. Brush a baking sheet with olive oil. Combine the tomatoes with a small amount of olive oil and toss to coat. Roast on the baking sheet for 10 minutes. Add to the potatoes and toss to coat. Flake the tuna over the salad. Add the anchovy fillets, capers and olives and mix gently. Tear the basil leaves and scatter over the salad. Serve immediately.

heirloom tomato salad

MAKES 4 TO 8 SERVINGS

1 cup currant tomatoes or grape tomatoes, or halved cherry tomatoes or pear tomatoes
1/2 cup chopped green onions
1/3 cup extra-virgin olive oil
Salt and pepper to taste
10 assorted color heirloom tomatoes, cored and thinly sliced

1 small red onion, sliced paper-thin
3 ribs celery, sliced thinly on the diagonal
1 1/2 cups coarsely crumbled blue cheese
8 (1/2-inch-thick) slices crusty bread
4 large garlic cloves, cut into halves
3 tablespoons extra-virgin olive oil

Preheat the grill to medium-high. Combine the currant tomatoes, green onions and 1/3 cup olive oil in a large bowl and toss to combine. Season with salt and pepper. Overlap the heirloom tomatoes in concentric circles on a platter, alternating colors. Scatter the red onion and celery over the heirloom tomatoes. Top with the green onion mixture. Sprinkle with the cheese.

Rub the bread with the cut garlic. Brush with 3 tablespoons olive oil. Grill for 2 minutes on each side or until golden brown. Cut each slice into halves diagonally. Serve with the salad.

wilted spinach salad with shrimp

MAKES 4 SERVINGS

12 large shrimp (size 16 to 20)
1 cup Dijon mustard
4 slices bacon
2 tablespoons cider vinegar
1 1/2 cups apple cider
1 teaspoon sugar
1 teaspoon Dijon mustard

1 tablespoon olive oil
2 (6-ounce) packages fresh spinach,
    stems removed
2 large tomatoes, chopped (use heirloom
    tomatoes if available)
1 (16-ounce) can cannellini beans
2 hard-cooked eggs, chopped

Peel and devein the shrimp, leaving the tails on. Marinate the shrimp in 1 cup Dijon mustard for 20 minutes. Cook the bacon in a sauté pan until crisp-cooked; drain, reserving 2 tablespoons of the bacon drippings in the saucepan. Crumble the bacon. Reheat the sauté pan and cook the shrimp for 3 to 5 minutes.

Combine the vinegar, apple cider, sugar, 1 teaspoon Dijon mustard and the olive oil in a small saucepan and whisk to blend. Heat to boiling over high heat, whisking constantly. Reduce the heat to low.

Place the spinach in a large bowl. Add the hot dressing 1 tablespoon at a time until the spinach is slightly wilted, tossing to coat. (You may not need all of the dressing.) Divide the spinach mixture evenly among four plates. Combine the tomatoes and beans in a bowl. Divide evenly between the plates. Top each salad with the bacon, eggs and three shrimp.

meat
& poultry
served

Fort Lauderdale has two seasons . . . hot summers and warm, mild winters. Temperatures in this tropical climate average 82 degrees with approximately three thousand hours of sunshine each year. There is no questioning the year-round appeal for those hiding from chilly snow and ice.

marinated grilled beef tenderloin

MAKES 2 TO 4 SERVINGS

3/4 cup soy sauce	2 green onions, sliced
1/2 cup sugar	1 to 2 garlic cloves, minced
1/2 cup toasted sesame seeds	1/4 teaspoon pepper
1 teaspoon ground ginger	2 (8-ounce) beef tenderloin fillets, or
1/4 cup canola oil	1 pound whole flank steak
1/4 cup all-purpose flour	

Combine the soy sauce, sugar, sesame seeds, ginger, canola oil, flour, green onions, garlic and pepper in a bowl and mix well. Pour the mixture over the beef in a glass baking dish. Marinate in the refrigerator for 3 hours or longer. Grill to the desired degree of doneness.

To make a sauce, reserve some of the soy sauce mixture before pouring over the beef. Heat in a saucepan and pour into a gravy boat.

Photo, page 72: Herb-Crusted Rack of Lamb, recipe page 81; Roasted Garlic Mashed Potatoes, recipe page 120

fantastic fillet

1/2 cup olive oil
1/2 cup soy sauce
1/2 cup sherry or marsala
1 tablespoon chopped grated fresh ginger
1 garlic clove, scored

1/2 teaspoon dried basil, or a handful of
fresh basil, minced
1 (5- to 7-pound) beef fillet
1 cup honey
1 teaspoon freshly ground pepper
1/2 cup orange juice

Combine the olive oil, soy sauce, sherry, ginger, garlic and basil in a bowl. Arrange the beef in a glass dish and pour the mixture over it. Cover with plastic wrap. Marinate in the refrigerator for 6 to 8 hours, turning every 2 hours and basting with the marinade.

Preheat the oven to 500 degrees. Remove the beef to a roasting pan, reserving the marinade. Combine the reserved marinade with the honey, pepper and orange juice in a bowl and mix well. Pour over the beef and roast for 10 minutes. Reduce the temperature to 400 degrees. Baste the beef with the marinade and roast for 10 minutes longer. Reduce the heat to 350 degrees. Baste the beef with the marinade and roast for 10 minutes longer or to the desired degree of doneness. Arrange on a serving platter. Pour the remaining marinade over the beef and let stand for 10 to 15 minutes before carving.

Ask your butcher to trim the ends of the beef fillet and tie it for roasting. The fillet should be about 1 foot long. To serve for a cocktail buffet, cut into thin slices and serve with miniature rolls. To serve for dinner, cut into 1/2-inch-thick slices.

John Offerdahl is a five-time Pro Bowl middle linebacker for the Miami Dolphins who spent his entire eight-year (1986–1993) NFL career here in South Florida. His most recent success has been off the field and in the kitchen of his popular chain of restaurants, Offerdahl's Café Grill.

baja steak

MAKES 2 TO 4 SERVINGS

Steak Rub and Steak
1/2 cup chili powder
1/2 cup ground fennel
1/4 cup garlic salt
1/4 cup lemon pepper
2 pounds steak

Sauce
2 cups mayonnaise
3 tablespoons Worcestershire sauce
3 tablespoons lemon juice

Dash of garlic powder
1 1/2 teaspoons garlic salt
1 tablespoon lemon pepper

Assembly
4 cups cooked rice
1 head romaine, chopped
1 (15-ounce) can black beans, heated
2 tomatoes, chopped
1/4 cup sliced scallions

For the steak rub, combine the chili powder, fennel, garlic salt and lemon pepper in a bowl. Rub over the steaks. Chill in the refrigerator for 8 hours or longer. For the sauce, beat the mayonnaise, Worcestershire sauce, lemon juice, garlic powder, garlic salt and lemon pepper in a bowl with an electric mixer.

Preheat the grill. Grill the steak to the desired degree of doneness. Slice the steak. Layer the rice, lettuce, black beans, tomatoes, and steak on four plates. Top with scallions and sauce.

This recipe is from the kitchen of John Offerdahl.

oven porcupines

1 pound ground beef
1/2 cup uncooked instant rice
1/2 cup water
1/3 cup chopped onion
1 teaspoon salt
1/2 teaspoon celery salt

1/8 teaspoon garlic powder
1/8 teaspoon pepper
1 (18-ounce) can tomato sauce
1 cup water
2 1/2 teaspoons Worcestershire sauce

Preheat the oven to 375 degrees. Combine the ground beef, rice, 1/2 cup water, the onion, salt, celery salt, garlic powder and pepper in a bowl and mix well. Shape the mixture into balls. Arrange in an ungreased baking dish. Stir together the tomato sauce, 1 cup water and the Worcestershire sauce. Pour over the meatballs, covering them completely. Cover the dish with foil. Bake for 30 minutes. Uncover and bake for 30 minutes longer.

taco pie

1 1/2 pounds ground beef
1 envelope taco seasoning mix
Nonstick cooking spray
4 (10-inch) flour tortillas
2 cups sour cream

2 cups (8 ounces) shredded Mexican blend
    cheese or Cheddar cheese
1 (16-ounce) jar salsa
Shredded lettuce for garnish
Chopped tomato for garnish
Jalapeño chiles for garnish

Preheat the oven to 350 degrees. Brown the ground beef with the taco seasoning mix in a sauté pan according to the package directions; drain. Spray a 9-inch pie dish with cooking spray. Arrange a tortilla in the bottom. Cover with the sour cream. Layer one-third of the ground beef, 1/4 cup of the cheese and 1/3 cup of the salsa over the sour cream. Top with another tortilla. Continue the layering process with the sour cream, ground beef, cheese, salsa and tortillas. End with a tortilla topped with sour cream and cheese. Cover with foil. Bake for 15 minutes. Remove the foil and bake for 5 minutes longer or until the cheese is melted. Slice and serve with additional sour cream and salsa. Garnish with lettuce, tomato and jalapeño chiles.

South Florida is a key region for the production of pomegranates. Pomegranate juice has recently gained mainstream popularity. When reduced with sugar, pomegranate juice makes grenadine. Grenadine is the super-sweet, red liquid used to make cocktails, including the Shirley Temple.

pork chops and cabbage with cider gravy

MAKES 4 TO 6 SERVINGS

Pork and Cabbage

4 to 6 pork chops, cut $1/2$ inch thick
3 cups shredded cabbage
$1/2$ to $3/4$ cup baby carrots, cut into halves
$3/4$ cup onion wedges
1 cup apple cider
2 to 3 teaspoons prepared horseradish
1 cup cored sliced red or green apple

Cider Gravy

$1/4$ cup apple cider
1 tablespoon cornstarch
1 teaspoon instant beef bouillon granules
$1/4$ teaspoon pepper

For the pork chops and cabbage, trim the fat from the pork. Coat a large, cold sauté pan with nonstick cooking spray. Brown the pork in the sauté pan over medium heat for about 4 minutes on each side. Add the cabbage, carrots, onion, cider and horseradish. bring to a boil; reduce the heat and cover. Simmer for 8 to 10 minutes or until cabbage is tender. Add the apple and cook for 2 to 3 minutes longer. Remove the pork, vegetables and apple to a platter, reserving the liquid in the sauté pan. Keep warm.

For the gravy, add the cider to the sauté pan along with the cornstarch, bouillon granules and pepper. Cook for about 2 minutes or until thickened and bubbly, stirring constantly. Serve with the pork.

adobo pork

2 pounds pork loin, cut into chunks
1 head garlic, crushed
1/2 cup soy sauce
1 teaspoon ground pepper

3/4 cup white vinegar
1 tablespoon vegetable oil
2 bay leaves

Combine the pork with the garlic, soy sauce, pepper and vinegar in a large pan. Marinate for 2 hours in the refrigerator. Place the pan over low heat and cook for 45 minutes or until the pork is tender. Remove the garlic. Heat the oil in a medium sauté pan. Add the garlic and sauté until brown. Add the pork and sauté until brown; drain. Add the cooking liquid to the pork and garlic. Add the bay leaves and simmer for 10 minutes.

pork tonnato

MAKES 8 TO 10 SERVINGS

2 pork tenderloins (up to 3 pounds total)
Montreal Chicken seasoning to taste
1/2 cup extra-virgin olive oil
1 (6-ounce) can Italian tuna in oil, undrained
4 anchovy fillets, chopped
2 tablespoons fresh lemon juice

3 tablespoons drained capers
1 cup mayonnaise
Salt and pepper to taste
1 lemon, sliced
Chopped parsley for garnish

Bring the pork to room temperature. Preheat the oven to 325 degrees. Season with chicken seasoning. Arrange on a greased roasting pan. Roast for 35 to 45 minutes or until a meat thermometer inserted into the thickest portion registers 140 degrees. Remove from the oven and cover with foil. Let stand for up to 2 hours.

Combine the olive oil, tuna, anchovy fillets, lemon juice, capers and mayonnaise in a blender. Process until well combined. Season with salt and pepper. Chill in the refrigerator. Cut the pork tenderloins into slices. Spread thoroughly with the sauce. Garnish with lemon slices and parsley.

For a different flavor, substitute veal or turkey.

pork tenderloin with mustard sauce

Mustard Sauce

1/3 cup mayonnaise

1/3 cup sour cream

1 tablespoon prepared mustard

1 tablespoon Dijon mustard

1 tablespoon grated onion

1 1/4 teaspoons prepared horseradish

1 tablespoon tarragon vinegar

Salt and pepper to taste

Pork and Marinade

1/2 cup soy sauce

2 tablespoons grated onion

2 garlic cloves, minced

1 tablespoon tarragon vinegar

1/4 teaspoon cayenne pepper

1/4 cup water

1 to 2 whole pork tenderloins

3 to 6 slices bacon

For the mustard sauce, combine the mayonnaise, sour cream, prepared mustard, Dijon mustard, onion, horseradish, vinegar, salt and pepper in a bowl. Refrigerate for 8 hours or longer.

For the pork and marinade, combine the soy sauce, onion, garlic, vinegar, cayenne pepper and water in a large sealable plastic bag. Add the pork. Chill in the refrigerator for 8 hours or longer. Preheat the oven to 325 degrees. Arrange the tenderloins in a roasting pan. Pour the marinade over them. Top each tenderloin with three slices of the bacon. Bake for 1 hour. Serve with the mustard sauce.

rosemary-scented lamb rigatoni

Olive oil for sautéing

2 garlic cloves, chopped

6 ounces lamb, cut into thin strips

1/2 red bell pepper, cut into strips

2 ounces dry white wine or chicken stock

16 ounces crushed tomatoes

1 rosemary sprig

2 tablespoons heavy cream

Salt and pepper to taste

8 ounces rigatoni, cooked and drained

2 ounces grated Parmesan cheese

1 tablespoon chopped rosemary

1 tablespoon chopped sage

1 tablespoon chopped oregano

Heat a small amount of olive oil in a sauté pan and add the garlic, lamb and bell pepper. Sauté for about 7 minutes or until lamb is tender. Add the wine. Cook until the liquid is almost evaporated. Add the tomatoes and rosemary sprig. Simmer for 15 minutes. Stir in the cream, salt and pepper. Cook until heated through. Toss with the rigatoni. Sprinkle with the cheese, 1 tablespoon rosemary, the sage and oregano.

herb-crusted rack of lamb

1 tablespoon finely minced garlic

1 teaspoon chopped fresh thyme

1 teaspoon finely chopped fresh chives

1 teaspoon minced fresh mint

1/2 cup Dijon mustard

3/4 cup bread crumbs

2 tablespoons olive oil

2 racks of lamb, 4 to 5 ribs each and frenched to eye of meat (1 1/2 pounds total)

Salt and pepper to taste

1 1/2 cups beef stock

1 1/2 cups red wine

2 1/2 teaspoons minced fresh mint

2 tablespoons butter

4 ounces heavy cream

1/4 cup pine nuts

1 tablespoon butter

9 ounces spinach, washed and stems removed

Preheat the oven to 425 degrees. Combine the garlic, thyme, chives, 1 teaspoon mint and the Dijon mustard in a bowl. Whisk to blend. Combine the bread crumbs and olive oil in a bowl. Toast in a sauté pan over medium heat for 3 to 5 minutes or until light brown and beginning to hold together, stirring constantly. Return to the bowl.

Wrap the lamb bones in foil, leaving the meat uncovered. Season with salt and pepper. Hold the meat by the bone upright and coat with the herb mixture. Coat with the bread crumb mixture, pressing lightly so the crumbs will adhere. Arrange the meat in a roasting pan, rounded side up. Roast for 25 to 30 minutes, turning once halfway through cooking. A meat thermometer inserted two inches into the center (but not touching the bone) should read 135 degrees for medium-rare and 125 for rare. Cool for 10 minutes. Cut into chops.

Bring the stock and wine to a boil in a sauté pan. Add 2 1/2 teaspoons mint and 2 tablespoons butter. Simmer for 10 minutes. Add the cream and cook for 5 minutes to reduce. Season with salt and pepper to taste. Strain the sauce.

Toast the pine nuts of a baking sheet in the oven for 5 minutes. Melt 1 tablespoon butter in a sauté pan over medium heat and add the spinach. Sauté the spinach, using tongs to stir, for 1 minute. Add the pine nuts and continue cooking and stirring for 1 minute.

Arrange the spinach in the middle of the plates. Drizzle the Dijon mustard sauce around the spinach. Arrange two or three chops bone side up on the spinach on each plate.

apricot brandy chicken

MAKES 4 SERVINGS

16 ounces bow tie pasta
Salt to taste
1/4 cup (1/2 stick) butter
1 cup chopped onion
4 to 8 ounces boneless skinless chicken breasts
1/2 cup all-purpose flour
1/4 cup (1/2 stick) butter

1 teaspoon fresh thyme leaves
1 1/2 cups apricot brandy
1 1/2 cups sour cream
Pepper to taste
4 ounces shaved Parmesan cheese
8 thyme sprigs

Cook the pasta in boiling salted water according to the package directions; drain. Heat 1/4 cup butter in a sauté pan and caramelize the onions; set aside. Coat the chicken with the flour. Heat 1/4 cup butter in a sauté pan and sauté the chicken until golden brown on one side. Turn the chicken and add the thyme leaves and caramelized onion. Cook for about 2 minutes. Pour in the brandy and cook until reduced by half. Add the sour cream and mix well. Add the pasta and bring to a simmer, taking care not to scorch. Season with salt and pepper. Cook for about 3 minutes or until heated through. Serve hot, garnished with cheese and thyme sprigs.

island chicken

MAKES 6 SERVINGS

1 1/2 teaspoons ground ginger
2 1/2 tablespoons brown sugar
Salt and pepper to taste
1 1/2 cups peanut oil
1 1/2 cups orange juice

1/3 cup lemon juice
1/3 cup lime juice
1 1/2 teaspoons crushed garlic
1 tablespoon soy sauce
6 boneless skinless chicken breasts

Combine the ginger, brown sugar, salt and pepper in a medium bowl. Add the peanut oil, orange juice, lemon juice, lime juice, garlic and soy sauce and mix well. Combine the marinade and chicken in an airtight container. Chill in the refrigerator or freeze until ready to use. Drain the marinade and reserve if grilling. Preheat the oven to 350 degrees. Bake the chicken for 45 to 60 minutes or grill over hot coals until cooked through. Serve with fried plantains, rice and black beans.

If grilling the chicken, bring the marinade to a boil and use it to baste the chicken.

mojo chicken

MAKES 2 SERVINGS

¼ teaspoon olive oil	¼ cup chopped tomato
2 chicken breasts	¼ cup chopped onion
Pinch of adobo seasoning	½ cup mojo criollo marinade
Pinch of salt	

Heat the olive oil in a pan over medium-high heat. Add the chicken. Season with adobo seasoning and salt and sear on both sides. Remove the chicken from the pan and cut into cubes.

Reduce the heat to medium and add the tomato and onion. Sauté until the onion is almost translucent. Return the chicken to the pan. Cook for 2 minutes or until the chicken is cooked through, stirring frequently. Add the mojo marinade. Cook, covered, for 5 minutes longer.

For a tasty alternative, substitute sirloin steak for the chicken.

citrus chicken

Citrus Marinade	Citrus Rub and Chicken
3 cups orange juice	1 tablespoon salt
1 cup grapefruit juice	1 teaspoon cracked pepper
1 teaspoon ground ginger	1 teaspoon garlic powder
1 teaspoon garlic powder	2 tablespoons sugar
1/4 teaspoon ground coriander	1 teaspoon paprika
2 bay leaves	1 teaspoon ground ginger
1 tablespoon peppercorns	1/2 teaspoon ground thyme
1/4 cup mushroom soy sauce	1/4 teaspoon ground cardamom
1/4 cup honey	1/2 teaspoon dry mustard
2 teaspoons salt	1 (3 1/2-pound) chicken
2 star anise	1/4 cup (1/2 stick) butter
2 cinnamon sticks, broken into halves	Orange or grapefruit slices for garnish

For the marinade, combine the orange juice, grapefruit juice, ginger, garlic powder, coriander, bay leaves, peppercorns, soy sauce, honey, salt, star anise and cinnamon sticks in a bowl and mix well.

For the rub, combine the salt, pepper, garlic powder, sugar, paprika, ginger, thyme, cardamom and dry mustard in a bowl and mix well.

Remove the giblets from the chicken. Truss the chicken. Combine the chicken and the marinade in a glass dish or sealable plastic bag. Marinate in the refrigerator for 4 hours or longer, rotating occasionally.

Preheat the oven to 450 degrees. Remove the chicken from the marinade. Spread butter all over the chicken. Coat the chicken with the citrus rub. Arrange the chicken breast side down in a roasting pan. Roast for 15 minutes. Reduce the heat to 325 degrees. Roast for 30 to 45 minutes longer. Turn chicken breast side up. Baste with the pan juices. Roast for 30 minutes or until juices run clear when the chicken is pierced with a fork.

chicken diablo

1/4 cup all-purpose flour

2 ounces Cajun seasoning

4 to 8 ounces boneless skinless chicken breasts

3 ounces olive oil

4 ounces julienned red onion

2 ounces julienned red bell pepper

2 ounces julienned yellow bell pepper

1 (25-ounce) jar marinara sauce

3 ounces heavy whipping cream

3 cups fresh multicolor five-cheese tortellini, cooked and drained

4 ounces shaved Parmesan cheese

Preheat the oven to 375 degrees. Combine the flour and Cajun seasoning in a bowl. Coat the chicken with the flour mixture. Heat half of the olive oil in a cast-iron skillet over medium heat. Blacken the chicken on each side for 5 minutes. Remove the chicken to a baking pan and bake until cooked through.

Heat the remaining olive oil in a skillet and add the onion and bell peppers. Sauté for 2 minutes or until tender-crisp. Stir in the marinara sauce and cook until heated through. Stir in the cream.

Cut the chicken into strips and place on top of pasta. Divide tortellini evenly among four to six plates. Finish the marinara sauce mixture. Garnish with cheese.

spicy mediterranean grilled chicken

1/2 cup salt

1/2 cup sugar

6 to 10 chicken pieces

3 tablespoons dried oregano

2 tablespoons fresh rosemary

3 tablespoons dried thyme

3 tablespoons salt

2 tablespoons red pepper flakes

3 tablespoons garlic powder

3 tablespoons onion powder

3 tablespoons dried tarragon

2 tablespoons lemon pepper

Combine the salt, sugar and chicken in a stockpot or large bowl with enough water to cover. Let stand for 4 hours. Combine the oregano, rosemary, thyme, salt, pepper flakes, garlic powder, onion powder, tarragon and lemon pepper in a small bowl.

Remove the chicken from the brine. Pat dry. Rub the chicken all over with the spice mixture. Grill over hot coals until cooked through.

pine nut-crusted chicken with balsamic tomato salsa

Balsamic Tomato Salsa

2 Roma tomatoes, chopped

$1/4$ cup chopped red onion

$1/4$ cup chopped celery

1 garlic clove, chopped

1 tablespoon balsamic vinegar

$1 1/2$ teaspoons extra-virgin olive oil

Chicken Cutlets

$1/4$ cup plain bread crumbs

3 tablespoons pine nuts

$1/2$ teaspoon salt

$1/2$ teaspoon pepper

$1 1/2$ pounds chicken cutlets

2 tablespoons olive oil

For the salsa, combine the tomatoes, onion, celery and garlic in a bowl. Add the vinegar and olive oil and mix well.

For the chicken, combine the bread crumbs, pine nuts, salt and pepper in a food processor. Pulse to chop the pine nuts and to combine. Pour the mixture into a shallow dish. Add the chicken and turn to coat with the bread crumb mixture.

Heat the olive oil in a sauté pan over medium-high heat. Add the chicken in batches and sauté for 2 to 3 minutes on each side or until golden brown and cooked through. Spoon salsa over the chicken to serve.

Chicken coating may also be made by chopping the pine nuts by hand and combining with the salt, pepper and bread crumbs.

P.S.

Fort Lauderdale is a major manufacturing and maintenance center for the world's yachts. It's a popular destination for yachting vacations because of our many canals and close proximity to the Caribbean. In addition, the Fort Lauderdale International Boat Show is the world's largest marine craft show, attracting more then 125,000 visitors each year.

salsa and saffron chicken

MAKES 4 SERVINGS

1 chicken, cut into pieces	2 cups hot water
1 (28-ounce) can crushed tomatoes	1 1/2 teaspoons pepper
1 (15-ounce) jar mild or hot salsa	1/4 teaspoon saffron
1 (15-ounce) can corn, drained	Salt to taste
3 ounces tomato paste	Hot cooked yellow rice

Arrange the chicken in a large pan such as a Dutch oven. Pour the tomatoes, salsa and corn over the chicken. Combine the tomato paste with the hot water and pour over the chicken. Season with the pepper, saffron and salt. Cook, covered, on the stove over medium heat for 1 hour. Uncover and stir gently, making sure all the chicken is covered with the sauce. Cook, covered, for 90 minutes longer.

P.S.

The City of Fort Lauderdale is named for a second Seminole War fort built in 1838. Major William Lauderdale led a detachment of Tennessee Volunteers to capture Seminole land. Altogether, three forts were named after Major Lauderdale: the first at the fork of the New River, the second at Tarpon Bend, and the largest is where the Bahia Mar Hotel now stands.

chicken tetrazzini

MAKES 4 TO 6 SERVINGS

2 teaspoons olive oil or canola oil

8 ounces penne or rigatoni pasta, cooked and drained

2 cups sliced fresh mushrooms

2 garlic cloves, minced

3 tablespoons butter or margarine

3 tablespoons all-purpose flour

2 cups chicken broth

1 cup double strained Greek yogurt

3 tablespoons sherry or white wine

2 teaspoons basil

1/8 teaspoon pepper

Dash of nutmeg

8 ounces cooked chicken breast, cut into 1/2-inch pieces

1/4 cup (1 ounce) freshly grated Parmesan cheese

Preheat the oven to 350 degrees. Coat a large baking dish with the olive oil. Combine the pasta and mushrooms in the baking dish. Heat the broth to near boiling.

Melt the butter in a nonstick saucepan. Stir in the flour. Add the hot broth gradually and cook until sauce boils and thickens, stirring constantly. Remove from heat and stir in the yogurt, sherry, basil, pepper, nutmeg and chicken. Pour the sauce over the pasta. Sprinkle with the cheese. Bake for 20 to 30 minutes or until heated through and light brown.

feta and tomato chicken

2 teaspoons olive oil
1 large Vidalia or sweet onion, chopped
2 garlic cloves, minced
1 pound skinless boneless chicken breasts,
cut into pieces

1 to 2 large tomatoes, chopped
8 ounces feta cheese
Salt and pepper to taste

Heat the olive oil in a sauté pan over medium-high heat. Add the onion and garlic and sauté until tender. Add the chicken and sauté until it is cooked through and no longer pink. Add the tomato and cheese. Cook until the cheese melts. Season with salt and pepper.

chicken marsala

16 ounces sliced fresh mushrooms
1/4 cup marsala
4 thin chicken breast cutlets
1/4 cup all-purpose flour
1 tablespoon olive oil
2 cups marsala

Salt and pepper to taste
Chopped parsley to taste
2 tablespoons all-purpose flour
Hot cooked noodles
Parsley for garnish

Sauté the mushrooms in 1/4 cup marsala in a sauté pan until tender; set aside. Dip the chicken into water and then coat with 1/4 cup flour. Heat the olive oil in a sauté pan and sauté the chicken for 3 minutes on each side. Add the mushrooms and 2 cups marsala. Simmer over medium heat for 5 minutes. Season with salt, pepper and parsley.

Combine 2 tablespoons flour with enough water to form a thin paste. Drizzle into the marsala sauce. Cook until thickened, stirring constantly. Serve the chicken and sauce over hot cooked noodles. Garnish with parsley.

yon mazeti

Vegetable oil for sautéing
1 cup chopped onion
2 green bell peppers, chopped
1 1/2 pounds ground pork
8 ounces mushrooms, sliced

16 ounces sharp Cheddar cheese, shredded
2 (10-ounce) cans tomato soup
Salt and pepper to taste
1 (12- to 16-ounce) package wide noodles

Heat a small amount of oil in a sauté pan and add the onion and bell peppers. Sauté until light brown. Add the pork and cook until brown and crumbly, stirring constantly. Add the mushrooms, cheese, soup, salt and pepper. Cook over low heat until the cheese is melted. Preheat the oven to 350 degrees. Cook the noodles according to the package directions; drain. Pour into a baking dish. Spoon the pork mixture over the noodles and mix well. Bake for 1 hour.

easy spiedini

2 pounds thin pork cutlets
1/2 cup Italian-style bread crumbs
Dash of salt
Dash of pepper
16 ounces Romano cheese, grated

1 tablespoon olive oil
Olive oil for sautéing
1 onion, sliced
1 (26-ounce) can Italian-style whole tomatoes

Preheat the oven to 350 degrees. Pound the cutlets until almost paper thin. Combine the bread crumbs, salt, pepper, cheese and 1 tablespoon olive oil and mix well. Heat a small amount of olive oil in a sauté pan and add the onion. Sauté until tender. Cut the tomatoes into small pieces and add to the onion. Sauté for a few minutes. Let cool. Spoon some of the bread crumb mixture over each cutlet. Add a small amount of the onion mixture. Roll to enclose the filling; secure each with a wooden pick. Arrange in a greased shallow casserole. Top with any remaining bread crumb mixture and onion mixture. Bake for 30 to 45 minutes or until the pork is cooked through.

Congressman Alcee Hastings, a native Floridian, represents District 23, which includes parts of Broward, Palm Beach, Hendry, Martin and St. Lucie counties. Congressman Hastings was first elected in 1992 and has been reelected seven times since.

chi-ve-po hungarian goulash

MAKES 6 SERVINGS

2 tablespoons bacon drippings or beef suet

8 ounces beef, cut into pieces

4 ounces veal, cut into pieces

4 ounces pork, cut into pieces

4 ounces chicken, cut into pieces

3 tablespoons all-purpose flour

1 large potato, cut into pieces

2 large onions, finely chopped

2 celery ribs, sliced

2 teaspoons paprika

2 garlic cloves

1 quart beef stock, burgundy or tomato juice, or a combination

Melt the drippings in a heavy sauté pan. Add the beef, veal, pork and chicken and sauté until light brown. Add the flour and mix well. Add the potato, onions, celery and paprika. Pierce each garlic clove with a wooden pick and add it to the sauté pan. Cook the mixture until tender, stirring constantly. Add the stock and cover. Simmer for about 2 hours or until tender. Remove and discard the garlic. Add boiling water if needed to thin the pan liquid to a gravy consistency.

This recipe is from the kitchen of Congressman Alcee Hastings.

paradise served

seafood
served

P.S.

Chef Carlos Fernandez is best known for his appearance on the second season of Bravo's hit show, "Top Chef." His local bistro, Hi-Life Café, is a Zagat-rated "Top 40" favorite where Chef Fernandez showcases award-winning (yet approachable) contemporary American cuisine. Stop channel-surfing and taste his talents at home!

bronzed tuna with black bean corn mélange

MAKES 4 SERVINGS

Black Bean Corn Mélange
1 (14-ounce) can black beans, cooked and drained
1 (8-ounce) can corn, cooked and drained
2 tablespoons minced fresh cilantro
1/2 teaspoon red wine vinegar
1/2 teaspoon lemon juice
1/2 red onion, finely chopped

Tuna Steaks
1/4 cup paprika
2 tablespoons Cajun seasoning
1 tablespoon sugar
Vegetable oil
4 to 8 ounces yellowfin tuna steaks
1 seedless cucumber, thinly sliced

For the mélange, combine the beans, corn, cilantro, vinegar, lemon juice and onion in a bowl and mix well. Chill for 2 to 12 hours. For the tuna, combine the paprika, Cajun seasoning and sugar. Coat tuna steaks on all sides with the mixture. Heat a small amount of oil in a large sauté pan over medium-high heat. Sear the tuna on both sides to rare. Arrange the tuna steaks and black bean corn mélange on a serving platter. Arrange the cucumber in a snakelike formation around the tuna.

This recipe is from the kitchen of Chef Carlos Fernandez.

Photo, page 92: *Bronzed Tuna with Black Bean Corn Mélange, recipe this page.*

Many of the fabulous fish found in dishes on menus across America are native to South Florida's waters, including tuna, dolphin, grouper, tilapia, snapper, bass, catfish, and sardines.

ritzy catfish

MAKES 4 SERVINGS

1 cup all-purpose flour
3 eggs
2 tablespoons Creole seasoning
2 sleeves butter crackers

4 (6- to 8-ounce) catfish fillets
Vegetable oil
1 lemon, cut into wedges

Spread the flour on a plate. Beat the eggs and Creole seasoning in a medium bowl. Pulse the crackers in a food processor until fine crumbs form. Spread the crumbs on a plate. Dip each catfish fillet in the flour, and then into the egg mixture. Roll in the cracker crumbs, pressing to adhere them to the surface.

Preheat a thin layer of oil in a sauté pan over medium-high heat for 3 to 4 minutes. Add the catfish, arranging them so they are not touching. Pan-fry each side for 3 to 5 minutes or until golden brown. Remove carefully. Serve with the lemon wedges.

paradise served

grouper with herb cheese sauce

2 pounds grouper, cut thin
1 bunch fresh curly parsley
1 (1/2-ounce) package fresh basil

1 cup mayonnaise
1 cup (4 ounces) grated Romano cheese
2 to 3 lemons

Rinse the fish and pat dry. Arrange on a large baking sheet with sides. Wash and dry the herbs. Remove and discard the stems. Mince in a food processor. Add the mayonnaise and cheese. Process until of a pastelike consistency. Spread the mixture over the fish, covering the entire surface. Bake for 20 to 30 minutes or until cooked through. The sauce will puff slightly and brown.

the big easy grouper

4 (6- to 8-ounce) grouper fillets
8 large shrimp, peeled and deveined (optional)
3/4 cup (1 1/2 sticks) butter, melted
2 tablespoons Worcestershire sauce
3 tablespoons fresh lemon juice

2 teaspoons chopped garlic
1 teaspoon black pepper
3/4 teaspoon white pepper
1 teaspoon salt

Preheat the oven to 350. Arrange the fish in a single layer in a shallow baking dish. Top each fillet with two shrimp. Combine the butter, Worcestershire sauce, lemon juice, garlic, black pepper, white pepper and salt in a bowl. Pour over the fish. Bake for 15 to 20 minutes or until the fish is cooked through. Makes extra sauce.

halibut with mango ginger sauce

MAKES 4 SERVINGS

Mango Ginger Sauce
2 mangoes, chopped
1 tablespoon Dijon mustard
1 tablespoon fresh lemon juice
1 (1-inch) peeled fresh ginger, minced
Dash of Worcestershire sauce
1 jalapeño chile, peeled, seeded and
chopped (optional)
Salt and pepper to taste

Halibut
4 (4- to 8-ounce) halibut fillets
Pinch of salt
Pinch of pepper
2 tablespoons olive oil

For sauce, combine the mangoes, Dijon mustard, lemon juice, ginger, Worcestershire sauce and jalapeño chile in a food processor. Pulse to combine. Season with salt and pepper. Spoon into a saucepan. Heat gently, but do not boil.

For the fish, preheat the oven to 350 degrees. Season the fish with salt and pepper. Heat an ovenproof sauté pan over medium heat. Add the olive oil. Sauté the fish, skin side up, for about 2 to 3 minutes. Turn and sauté 2 to 3 minutes longer. Bake for 2 to 4 minutes or until fish flakes easily with a fork.

Spoon some of the mango ginger sauce onto each plate. Serve the fish over the sauce.

tropical mahi mahi

1/3 cup chopped peach	Juice of 1 lemon
1/3 cup chopped melon	4 (6-ounce) mahi mahi steaks
1/3 cup chopped strawberries	1 tablespoon blackening seasoning
1/3 cup chopped mango	1 1/2 tablespoons butter
1/3 cup chopped cilantro	4 teaspoons honey

Combine the peach, melon, strawberries, mango, cilantro and lemon juice in a bowl and mix well. Let stand for 20 minutes. Season each steak with 3/4 teaspoon of the blackening seasoning. Heat a sauté pan over high heat. Add the butter and the fish. Let cook for 5 minutes. Turn the fish and drizzle with the honey. Cook until cooked through. Serve with the fruit salsa.

almond-encrusted yellowtail with ginger sauce

MAKES 4 SERVINGS

2 cups sliced almonds	2 to 3 pieces fresh ginger, peeled and thinly
1/4 cup all-purpose flour	sliced, or to taste
3 eggs, lightly beaten	Juice of 1 lime
4 yellowtail fillets or other flaky white fish	1 cup dry white wine
1/2 cup (1 stick) butter	1 cup heavy cream
2 tablespoons extra-virgin olive oil	Salt and pepper to taste
1/4 cup (1/2 stick) butter	1 lime, cut into wedges

Preheat the oven to 350 degrees. Combine the almonds and flour and spread on a flat pan. Coat each fillet with egg, and then coat with almond mixture.

Heat the olive oil and the butter in a sauté pan over medium to medium-high heat. Fry the fish on each side until a crust forms. Arrange the fish in a shallow baking dish. Bake in the oven for about 10 minutes, depending on the thickness of the fish. Heat the butter, ginger and lime juice in a sauté pan. Simmer gently for 5 minutes. Add the wine and cream and simmer until reduced by one-fourth. Top with the sauce and garnish with the lime wedges.

grilled salmon with soy and brown sugar sauce

Soy and Brown Sugar Sauce
1/2 cup (1 stick) butter
2 tablespoons brown sugar
3 tablespoons soy sauce
2 garlic cloves, crushed
2 tablespoons ketchup
1 tablespoon Worcestershire sauce
1 tablespoon dry or prepared mustard

Salmon
2 pounds salmon, in large pieces or
4 individual portions
1 large Vidalia onion, sliced
4 slices bacon, cut into halves
Nonstick cooking spray

For the sauce, combine the butter, brown sugar, soy sauce, garlic, ketchup, Worcestershire sauce and dry mustard in a saucepan. Cook until mixture is well blended and is near boiling, stirring constantly. Keep warm.

For the salmon, preheat the grill. Arrange a piece of bacon and a slice of onion on each piece of the salmon. Spray a grill topper with nonstick cooking spray. Arrange the fish onion side down. Grill for about 10 minutes. Turn and grill for about 10 minutes longer, depending on the thickness. Discard the bacon and onions. Serve with the warm sauce.

grilled tilapia in a pouch

4 (4- to 6-ounce) tilapia fillets or other
white fish fillets
1 large onion, cut into 1/4-inch slices

4 teaspoons lemon pepper
4 teaspoons extra-virgin olive oil
4 ice cubes

Preheat the grill to medium-low. Arrange four 18-inch-long sheets of foil on a work surface. Spray each with nonstick cooking spray. Arrange a tilapia fillet on each sheet. Arrange the onion on top of each fillet, dividing evenly among the four fillets. Sprinkle 1 teaspoon of the lemon pepper over each fillet. Drizzle 1 teaspoon of the olive oil over each fillet. Place an ice cube on each fillet. Fold the foil over the fillet. Seal all edges to create an airtight pouch. Grill the pouches for 10 to 15 minutes each or until fish flakes easily.

key west yellowtail snapper with tomato basil salsa

MAKES 1 SERVING

1 vine-ripe tomato, chopped	1 ounce white vinegar
1 teaspoon chopped garlic	Dash of Tabasco sauce
1 teaspoon chopped shallot	Salt and pepper to taste
5 basil leaves, chopped	6 to 8 ounces skinless yellowtail snapper fillet,
1 ounce extra-virgin olive oil	pin bone removed
Juice of 1 lemon	2 ounces olive oil seasoned with salt and pepper
1 tablespoon Key lime juice	

For the salsa, combine the tomato, garlic, shallot, basil, olive oil, lemon juice, lime juice, vinegar, Tabasco sauce, salt and pepper in a bowl and mix well. Preheat a grill or broiler. Coat the fish with the olive oil. Grill for 3 to 4 minutes on each side. Arrange the fish on a serving plate and top with the salsa.

This recipe is from the kitchen of Guy Harvey.

clams with chorizo broth

1 link chorizo, casings removed and sausage
thinly sliced
2 tablespoons butter
3 ounces white wine
4 ounces seafood stock
1 teaspoon minced garlic

1 pound baby clams
1 teaspoon finely chopped cilantro
8 ounces curly vermicelli
Fresh basil chiffonade
Salt and pepper to taste

Melt the butter in a large saucepan. Add the chorizo and sauté until the butter is the color of the chorizo. Add the wine, stock and garlic. Bring to a simmer and add the clams. Cook, covered, for 7 minutes or until the clams open.

Cook the pasta according to the package directions for 7 minutes; drain. Add to the saucepan with the clams. Add basil, salt and pepper and toss to combine.

This recipe is from the kitchen of Chef Carlos Fernandez.

P.S.

A self-taught chef, Cindy Hutson developed her passion for cooking at the age of nine. In 1999 Hutson opened Ortanique on the Mile in Coral Gables. It was immediately named Best New Restaurant by Esquire magazine. Ortanique "Cuisine of the Sun" restaurant offers authentic Caribbean cuisine with a fresh, light attitude.

west indian curried crab cakes

MAKES 8 SERVINGS

Mango Papaya Salsa
Chopped chives to taste
1/4 cup sugar
Juice of 3 limes
1/3 cup sliced scallion greens
1 teaspoon Scotch bonnet chile sauce, or to taste
1 cup chopped papaya
1 cup chopped mango
2 tablespoons chopped cilantro

Crab Cakes
3 eggs
1/2 cup mayonnaise

1 tablespoon whole grain mustard
1 tablespoon Worcestershire sauce
2 tablespoons Madras curry powder
2 scallions, green tops sliced
1/4 cup chopped red bell pepper
1/4 cup chopped yellow bell pepper
1/4 cup chopped red onion
1/4 cup parsley, chopped
1 cup panko
1 pound jumbo lump crab meat
Salt and pepper to taste
2 tablespoons butter

For the salsa, combine all ingredients in a bowl and mix well. For the crab cakes, beat the eggs, mayonnaise, mustard, Worcestershire sauce and curry powder in a large bowl. Let stand for 15 minutes. Preheat the oven to 400 degrees. Add the scallions, bell peppers, onion and parsley to the curry mixture and mix well. Add the panko, crab, salt and pepper and mix gently. Form into 3-ounce portions. Sear in hot butter in a sauté pan for 2 minutes on each side or until golden brown. Arrange in a baking pan. Bake for 8 to 10 minutes. Serve with the salsa.

This recipe is from the kitchen of Chef Cindy Hutson.

For two days every July, lobsters flood South Florida's waters for its short lobster season. It's good fortune to catch and bring home a few of these delicacies. Florida's spiny lobster, named for the short spines along its tail and body designed to ward off predators, is a favorite for its sweet and tender tail meat.

lobster and asparagus risotto

MAKES 6 TO 8 SERVINGS

5 tablespoons butter	2 cups arborio rice
2 pounds cooked lobster meat, cut into chunks	1/2 cup white wine
1/4 cup cooking sherry	8 cups (about) chicken stock
1/4 cup olive oil	12 asparagus spears, cut into pieces
2 tablespoons minced garlic	1/4 cup chopped Italian parsley
1 onion, chopped	1/4 cup (1 ounce) freshly grated
1 shallot, chopped	Parmesan cheese
1 leek, thinly sliced	Salt and pepper to taste

Heat a large sauté pan over medium-high heat. Add the butter and sauté the lobster for 5 minutes, stirring constantly. Add the sherry.

Heat a large saucepan over medium-high heat and add the olive oil. Add the garlic, onion, shallot and leek and sauté until translucent. Add the asparagus and sauté for 2 to 3 minutes. Add the rice and sauté for 3 minutes longer. Add the wine and cook until absorbed, stirring constantly. Add the stock 1/2 cup at a time and simmer until absorbed. Cook the rice until al dente. (You may not need all the stock, depending on the consistency of the rice.)

Add the lobster mixture and cook until the mixture is creamy and the liquid is absorbed, stirring frequently. Remove from the heat and add the parsley, cheese, salt and pepper. Serve immediately.

baby maine mussels with ginger lemon grass broth

MAKES 4 SERVINGS

3 pounds black mussels	1 cup dry white wine
1 (2-inch) piece fresh ginger, peeled, thinly sliced	1 cup fish stock
1 stalk lemon grass	1/4 cup (1/2 stick) butter
2 tablespoons olive oil	Salt and pepper to taste
2 tablespoons chopped garlic	1 bunch cilantro
	Juice of 1 lemon

Clean the mussels in cold water, removing any foreign objects from the shells. Tap them on the sink and discard those that remain wide open. Store in the refrigerator covered with a damp towel. Arrange the ginger slices in a single layer. Cut into fine strands. Peel the lemon grass and cut the tender portion of the stalk into 1-inch sticks. Smash the sticks lightly to release their flavor.

Sauté the ginger, lemon grass and garlic in the olive oil in a large sauté pan over medium-high heat for 1 minute. Add the mussels. Cook for 1 minute, stirring constantly. Deglaze the pan with the wine. Add the stock. Cook, covered, for 4 minutes. Add the butter and mix well. Season with salt and pepper. Cook until reduced by half. Add the cilantro and lemon juice. Divide the mussels and broth among individual serving bowls.

This recipe is from the kitchen of Chef Dean Max.

bourbon shrimp

32 jumbo shrimp, peeled and deveined
4 ounces prosciutto, thinly sliced
1/4 cup Dijon mustard

1/4 cup bourbon
1/4 teaspoon cayenne pepper
1/4 cup packed brown sugar

Wrap each shrimp with a slice of prosciutto. Skewer six to eight wrapped shrimp on a wooden skewer. Arrange in a single layer on a platter. Combine the Dijon mustard, bourbon and cayenne pepper in a small bowl. Brush the mixture over the shrimp. Chill in the refrigerator for 30 to 60 minutes. Preheat a gas or charcoal grill. Sift the brown sugar over both sides of the shrimp. Grill the shrimp for 2 to 3 minutes per side or until cooked through.

camarones enchilados

MAKES 4 SERVINGS

2 pounds shrimp
1/2 cup vegetable oil
1 onion, sliced
3 garlic cloves, chopped
1 large green bell pepper, sliced
1/2 cup chopped parsley
1 (8-ounce) can tomato sauce
1 (12-ounce) jar roasted red peppers, chopped
and liquid reserved

1/2 cup ketchup
1/2 cup dry wine
1 tablespoon vinegar
1 bay leaf
1 1/2 teaspoons salt
1 teaspoon pepper
1 teaspoon Tabasco sauce

Peel and devein the shrimp. Heat the oil in a large sauté pan and add the onion, garlic and bell pepper. Sauté for 1 to 2 minutes. Add the parsley, tomato sauce, undrained red peppers, ketchup, wine, vinegar, bay leaf, salt, pepper and Tabasco sauce. Simmer for 20 minutes. Add the shrimp and simmer for 8 minutes or until cooked through.

pan-seared sea scallops with vanilla key lime coconut sauce

MAKES 2 SERVINGS

1 (8- to 13-ounce) can coconut milk
1 shallot, chopped
1 garlic clove, chopped
1 tablespoon chopped fresh ginger
2 to 3 stalks fresh or dried lemon grass
3/4 cup white wine
1/2 cup rice wine vinegar
1/4 cup soy sauce
1 cup Key lime juice

1/2 cup chicken stock
1/2 to 3/4 cup clam juice
1 teaspoon sugar
1 tablespoon honey
1 teaspoon vanilla extract
1/2 cup (1 stick) unsalted butter
6 large white mushrooms, sliced
8 large sea scallops
Sea salt and pepper to taste

Cook the coconut milk, shallot, garlic, ginger and lemon grass in a saucepan over medium heat until tender. Add the wine, vinegar, soy sauce and lime juice. Cook until reduced by half. Add the stock, clam juice, sugar, honey and vanilla. Simmer over low to medium heat for about 20 minutes or until thickened. Strain into another pan. Season with salt and pepper.

Heat the butter in a sauté pan. Add the mushrooms and sauté until tender. Pat the scallops dry. Season with salt and add to the hot pan. Sear the scallops for approximately 2 minutes on each side or until brown, basting frequently. Layer the mushrooms and scallops on two plates. Spoon the sauce around the scallops.

This recipe is from the kitchen of Chef Robert Jacobs.

Fish living in trees? Yes! The mangrove killifish spends several months each year out of the water and hidden away inside South Florida's mangrove tree branches and trunks that have rotted.

fried shrimp

MAKES 8 TO 10 SERVINGS

36 ounces peanut oil
1 1/2 cups all-purpose flour
3 cups milk
2 eggs, lightly beaten

1 (10-ounce) package Louisiana Fish Fry
4 pounds fresh shrimp, peeled, deveined and
 tails on

Heat the oil in a deep fryer to 365 to 385 degrees. Preheat the oven to 200 degrees. Pour the flour into a bowl. Beat the eggs and milk in a second bowl. Pour the fish fry into a third bowl. Coat the shrimp lightly with flour. Dip into the egg mixture. Coat with the fish fry. Put the shrimp on a platter as they are coated.

Lower several shrimp at a time into the hot oil. Fry for 2 to 3 minutes or until golden brown. Keep the fried shrimp warm in the oven until all the shrimp are cooked.

healthy shrimp and vegetable bake

MAKES 4 SERVINGS

2 tablespoons olive oil	2 cups cherry tomatoes
1 cup coarsely chopped onion	2 cup sliced zucchini
3 garlic cloves, finely chopped	1 pound peeled deveined shrimp
1/2 teaspoon thyme	3 tablespoons olive oil
1 teaspoon dried basil, or 1 cup fresh basil, chopped	1/2 teaspoon salt
	1/2 teaspoon pepper
2 cups fresh mushroom halves	2 tablespoons chopped fresh parsley

Preheat the oven to 350 degrees. Heat 2 tablespoons olive oil in a sauté pan over medium heat. Add the onion and garlic and sauté until tender. Remove from the heat. Stir in thyme and basil.

Combine the mushrooms, tomatoes and zucchini in a 9x13-inch pan.

Stir the shrimp into the the onion mixture. Add to the baking pan. Drizzle with 3 tablespoons olive oil. Season with salt and pepper. Cover the pan with foil. Bake for 40 minutes. Sprinkle with the parsley before serving.

crab wrap sandwiches

1/2 head romaine, chopped

3/4 cup chopped red onion

3/4 cup chopped red, green and yellow bell peppers

2 tablespoons cilantro leaves

1 teaspoon Old Bay seasoning

1/2 cup olive oil

1/4 cup balsamic vinegar

1 pound lump crab meat

6 flour tortillas

1/2 to 1 cup sour cream

Combine the lettuce, onion, 1/2 cup of the bell peppers, the cilantro, Old Bay seasoning, olive oil and vinegar in a bowl. Flake the crab meat into the mixture. Spread each tortilla with a small amount of sour cream. Fill with crab mixture. Roll to enclose the filling, securing with wooden picks. Cut each roll into halves. Stand wraps on end on serving plates. Sprinkle with the remaining 1/4 cup bell peppers.

roasted greek shrimp wrap

MAKES 6 SERVINGS

1 1/2 pounds shrimp, peeled and deveined

3 ounces olive oil

Salt and pepper to taste

2 to 3 heads Boston or Bibb lettuce

4 ounces crumbled tomato-basil flavor feta cheese

1 pint cherry tomatoes, chopped

2 cucumbers, seeded and chopped

High-quality balsamic vinegar

Preheat the oven to 400 degrees. Arrange the shrimp in a single layer on a rimmed baking sheet. Drizzle with the olive oil. Season with salt and pepper. Bake for 6 minutes.

Start a wrap by setting a lettuce leaf on a plate. Layer four or five shrimp, 1 teaspoon of the cheese, 1 teaspoon of the tomatoes and 1 teaspoon of the cucumber over the lettuce. Drizzle with the vinegar. Roll to enclose the filling. Repeat with the remaining ingredients.

Soft taco shells may be substituted for the lettuce leaves.

seafood quesadillas with mango lime salsa

MAKES 4 SERVINGS

Mango Lime Salsa

1 mango, chopped
1/4 cup chopped red onion
2 tablespoons chopped cilantro
1 large tomato, chopped
Juice of 1 lime
1/4 to 1/2 teaspoon red pepper flakes, or
chopped jalapeño chile to taste
(optional)

Seafood Quesadillas

1 pound lobster, cooked, cut into 1/2-inch cubes
8 ounces petite salad shrimp, peeled, deveined
and cooked
8 ounces cooked or canned lump crab meat
Salt and freshly cracked pepper to taste
4 large flour tortillas
2 cups (8 ounces) shredded Monterey
Jack cheese
Sour cream

For the salsa, combine the mango, onion, cilantro, tomato, lime juice and pepper flakes in a bowl and mix well. Chill in the refrigerator until serving time.

For the quesadillas, combine the lobster, shrimp and crab in a large bowl. Season with salt and pepper and mix well. Heat a large skillet or electric grill to medium heat. Place a tortilla in the skillet. Spread half of the tortilla with one-fourth of the seafood mixture. Sprinkle 1/4 cup of the cheese over the seafood. Fold the tortilla over the filling. Heat until the cheese is melted. Repeat with the remaining tortillas, seafood mixture and cheese. Cut each quesadilla into four pieces. Sprinkle each serving with some of the remaining cheese. Serve with sour cream and the mango lime salsa.

P.S.

Built in 1905, Fort Lauderdale's New River Inn was Broward County's first tourist hotel. It now serves as the Old Fort Lauderdale Museum of History, housing one of Florida's most important collections of state and local history, including rare oral histories of pioneer life in southeast Florida.

red curry seafood

MAKES 8 SERVINGS

4 ounces red curry paste	1/4 cup chopped fresh cilantro
4 (13-ounce) cans coconut milk	1 1/3 cups water
1/2 cup fish sauce	2 1/2 pounds shrimp, peeled and deveined
1/2 cup packed brown sugar	12 ounces sea scallops
1/4 cup chopped fresh basil	1 pound lobster, grouper or calamari

Simmer the curry paste and the coconut milk in a stockpot for 5 minutes. Add the fish sauce, brown sugar, basil, cilantro and water. Simmer for 10 minutes, stirring occasionally. Stir in the shrimp, scallops and lobster. Cook for 3 to 4 minutes or until opaque.

Jasmine rice makes a delicious complement to this recipe.

sides
& pasta
served

artichoke and cheese squares

3 tablespoons sliced green onions
1 (14-ounce) can artichoke hearts, drained
and chopped
1/4 cup parsley
2 eggs
2 egg whites

3/4 cup (3 ounces) shredded low-fat
Swiss cheese
1/2 cup plain nonfat yogurt
1/2 cup fine dry bread crumbs
1/4 teaspoon salt

Preheat the oven to 350 degrees. Spray a small nonstick sauté pan with nonstick cooking spray. Heat over medium-high heat. Add the green onions and sauté for 3 minutes. Remove from the heat. Add the artichoke hearts and parsley and mix well. Beat the eggs and egg whites in a large bowl with a wire whisk. Add the cheese, yogurt, bread crumbs and salt and mix well. Add the artichoke mixture and mix well. Spread the mixture in a greased 9x9-inch baking pan. Bake for 20 minutes or until set. Cut into squares. Remove to a serving tray. Serve warm.

blue cheese green bean toss

MAKES 6 TO 8 SERVINGS

1/4 cup wine vinegar
1 teaspoon dried basil
1 teaspoon minced garlic
1 teaspoon oregano
1/4 cup chopped parsley
2/3 cup plus 2 tablespoons olive oil

1 1/2 pounds fresh green beans, cut into
2-inch pieces
1 1/2 cups water
1/2 teaspoon each garlic salt and pepper
2 cups halved cherry tomatoes
1 cup crumbled blue cheese

Combine the vinegar, basil, garlic, oregano, parsley and olive oil in a bowl. Combine the beans and water in a saucepan and bring to a boil. Reduce the heat and simmer, covered, for 12 to 15 minutes or until tender-crisp; drain. Combine the beans, garlic salt, pepper and tomatoes in a large serving bowl and mix well. Fold in the cheese. Add the vinegar mixture and toss to combine.

Photo, page 112: *Blue Cheese Green Bean Toss, recipe this page*

broccoli bake

3 (10-ounce) packages frozen broccoli
1 cup (4 ounces) shredded sharp
Cheddar cheese
1 (10-ounce) can cream of mushroom soup
1 (10-ounce) can cream of chicken soup

1/2 cup mayonnaise or mayonnaise-type
salad dressing
2 cups soft bread cubes (torn by hand)
3 tablespoons melted margarine

Preheat the oven to 375 degrees. Cook the broccoli according to the package directions, omitting the salt; drain. Combine the cheese, soups and mayonnaise in a large bowl. Add the broccoli and mix well. Spoon the mixture into a 9x13-inch baking dish. Combine the bread cubes and margarine in a bowl. Spread over the casserole. Bake for 30 minutes or until mixture bubbles and bread is brown.

You may substitute fresh broccoli or use a mixture of half broccoli and half cauliflower.

celery casserole

MAKES 8 SERVINGS

4 cups sliced celery
Salt to taste
1 (10-ounce) can cream of
celery soup
1/2 cup milk

1/4 cup butter cracker crumbs
1/2 cup (1 stick) butter, melted
1 cup butter cracker crumbs
1/2 cup sliced pecans
Salt and pepper to taste

Preheat the oven to 350 degrees. Cook the celery in lightly salted water in a saucepan for 8 minutes; drain. Combine the celery with the soup, milk and 1/2 cup cracker crumbs. Spoon into a 2-quart baking dish.

Combine the butter, 1 cup cracker crumbs and the pecans in a bowl. Spread over the celery mixture. Bake, uncovered, for 1 hour.

corn pudding in a jiffy

MAKES 8 TO 10 SERVINGS

1/2 cup (1 stick) butter, melted	1 (15-ounce) can cream-style corn
2 eggs	1 (15-ounce) can whole kernel corn, drained
1 cup sour cream	1 (8-ounce) package corn muffin mix

Preheat the oven to 350 degrees. Combine the butter, eggs and sour cream in a large bowl and mix well. Add the cream-style corn, whole kernel corn and the muffin mix and mix well. Spoon into a 9x12-inch baking dish. Bake for 45 minutes.

latin lentils

1/4 teaspoon olive oil
1/4 cup chopped tomatoes
1/4 cup chopped onion
1/4 teaspoon ground bay leaf
1/4 teaspoon ground cumin

Dash of paprika
1 (15-ounce) can lentils
1 packet Goya Sazon with coriander
and annatto

Heat the olive oil in a saucepan. Add the tomatoes, onion, bay leaf, cumin and paprika and sauté until the onion is semitranslucent. Add the lentils and Goya Sazon and mix well. Cook, covered, for 8 minutes. Serve hot.

vidalia onion pie

MAKES 8 TO 10 SERVINGS

1 cup butter cracker crumbs
1/4 cup (1/2 stick) butter, melted
2 tablespoons butter
1 large Vidalia onion, thinly sliced (about 2 cups)
2 eggs, beaten
3/4 cup milk

3/4 teaspoon salt
Dash of pepper
1/4 cup (1 ounce) shredded sharp
Cheddar cheese
Dash of paprika
Dash of dried parsley

Preheat the oven to 350 degrees. Combine the cracker crumbs and butter in a bowl. Press over the bottom of an 8-inch pie plate. Heat the butter in a large sauté pan and add the onion. Sauté until translucent. Spoon the onion into the pie shell. Combine the eggs, milk, salt and pepper in a bowl and mix well. Pour over the onions. Sprinkle with the cheese, paprika and parsley. Bake for 30 minutes. Serve warm.

Rick Shaw has the longest career of any disc jockey in South Florida and is a local legend for having entertained South Floridians for forty-seven years. Now retired from radio, he continues to give back to the community as president of the Majic Children's Fund, founded in 1988.

super stuffed peppers

MAKES 6 SERVINGS

6 green bell peppers
2 tablespoons vegetable oil
1 cup chopped onion
1/2 cup chopped green bell pepper
1 pound ground beef
1 tablespoon minced garlic
1/4 cup chopped parsley
3/4 teaspoon salt
Pinch of red pepper flakes
1/2 teaspoon black pepper
2 cups cooked elbow macaroni
1 (8-ounce) can tomato sauce

Parboil 6 bell peppers in water for 2 to 3 minutes; drain. Heat the oil in a large sauté pan and add the onion and 1/2 cup bellpepper. Sauté for 3 minutes. Add the ground beef, garlic, parsley, salt, red pepper flakes and black pepper. Cook for 15 minutes. Add the macaroni and tomato sauce.

Preheat the oven to 350 degrees. Cut the tops off of the 6 bell peppers. Remove the seeds and membranes. Stuff the ground beef mixture into the bell peppers. Pour 1/8 inch of water into the bottom of a baking dish. Arrange the bell peppers in the dish. Bake for 30 to 35 minutes.

This recipe is from the kitchen of Rick Shaw.

potato herb gratin

3 tablespoons olive oil

6 thick garlic cloves, chopped

2 cups thinly sliced onions

Salt and pepper to taste

2 tablespoons chopped fresh thyme

2 tablespoons chopped fresh rosemary

Olive oil for brushing

2 pounds Yukon Gold potatoes, peeled and cut into 1/2-inch-thick rounds

1 teaspoon salt

3/4 teaspoon coarsely ground pepper

6 thick slices Swiss cheese

6 ounces shaved Parmesan cheese

1 1/2 cups milk

2 ounces shaved Parmesan cheese

Dash of chopped fresh Italian parsley

Preheat the oven to 425 degrees. Heat 3 tablespoons olive oil in a large skillet over medium heat. Add the garlic and onions. Sprinkle with salt and pepper. Sauté for 8 minutes. Add the thyme and rosemary. Sauté for 2 minutes. Set aside.

Brush a baking dish with olive oil. Arrange half of the potatoes in an overlapping pattern in the dish. Sprinkle with 1/4 teaspoon of the salt and 1/4 teaspoon of the pepper. Top with half of the onion mixture, four slices of Swiss cheese and 3 ounces of the Parmesan cheese. Continue layering with the remaining potatoes. Pour the milk over them. Continue layering with the remaining onion mixture, salt, pepper, Swiss cheese and Parmesan cheese.

Bake, covered with foil, for 35 minutes. Bake, uncovered, for 15 minutes longer or until tender and golden brown. Turn off the oven. Top with 2 ounces Parmesan cheese. Leave in the oven for 3 minutes. Let stand for 10 minutes. Garnish with parsley.

roasted garlic mashed potatoes

4 garlic bulbs
3 ounces olive oil
8 pounds Yukon Gold potatoes, peeled
3/4 cup (1 1/2 sticks) butter
1 1/2 cups warm milk

3 tablespoons kosher salt
1/2 teaspoon white pepper
1/2 cup sour cream
Chopped fresh Italian parsley

Preheat the oven to 425 degrees. Cut enough of the top from each garlic bulb to expose the cloves. (The side cloves may need to be cut individually to expose them.) Place the whole bulbs in a small roasting pan. Drizzle the olive oil over the garlic. Cover the pan with foil. Roast for 30 to 40 minutes. Let cool for a few minutes. Remove each clove with a paring knife. Place the cloves on a cutting board. Mash the cloves to a paste with the flat side of a knife.

Combine the potatoes and water to cover in a stockpot over medium heat. Bring to a boil and cook for 20 minutes or until a knife inserted in the potato slides in easily. Do not overcook. Drain in a colander and let cool.

Combine the potatoes, garlic paste, butter, half of the milk, the salt and pepper and beat with an electric mixer set at low speed. Add the remaining milk and the sour cream and mix well. Do not overmix or beat at high speed. Garnish with parsley.

Commissioner Cindi Hutchinson is a Fort Lauderdale native. Elected to the Fort Lauderdale City Commission in 2000, she has served as vice mayor in 2002 and again in 2006. She makes "Sunday dinner" for seventeen family members nearly every week! Cindi loves convenient comfort foods, and this dish is her favorite because it is so simple to prepare before entertaining.

drive 'em wild potatoes

MAKES 12 SERVINGS

4 pounds russet potatoes	8 bacon slices, crisp-cooked and crumbled
(about 6 large potatoes)	3 tablespoons chopped fresh chives
1 cup sour cream	3 cups (12 ounces) shredded mozzarella cheese
1/4 cup (1/2 stick) butter or margarine	1/2 cup (2 ounces) shredded Swiss cheese

Peel and quarter the potatoes. Cook in boiling water in a saucepan until fork tender; drain. Return the potatoes to the saucepan. Add the sour cream and butter. Mash with a potato masher or beat with an electric mixer. Stir in the bacon and 2 tablespoons of the chives. Stir in the mozzarella cheese. Spoon the mixture into a lightly greased 3-quart baking dish. Sprinkle evenly with the Swiss cheese. Bake for 20 to 25 minutes or until the cheese is lightl brown and the potatoes are heated through. Sprinkle with the remaining chives.

This recipe is from the kitchen of Commissioner Cindi Hutchinson.

sawgrass spinach squares

1/4 cup (1/2 stick) butter
3 eggs
1 cup all-purpose flour
1 cup milk
1 teaspoon salt

1 teaspoon baking powder
Onion powder to taste
2 (9-ounce) packages frozen spinach, thawed
16 ounces sharp Cheddar cheese, shredded

Preheat the oven to 325 degrees. Put the butter in a 9x12-inch baking dish and place in the oven to melt.

Combine the eggs, flour, milk, salt and baking powder in a bowl and whisk to blend. Add the onion powder and mix well. Squeeze the excess cooking liquid from the spinach. Add the spinach and cheese to the egg mixture and mix well.

Spread the mixture over the melted butter. Sprinkle with additional onion powder. Bake for 30 to 35 minutes or until the top begins to brown.

maple butternut squash

MAKES 6 TO 8 SERVINGS

3 medium to large butternut squash
1/2 cup (1 stick) butter
10 ounces pure grade A maple syrup

3/4 cup packed brown sugar
10 ounces goat cheese (optional)

Preheat the oven to 375 degrees. Cut each squash into halves lengthwise. Arrange cut side up on two foil-lined roasting pans. Put a pat of butter onto the cut side of each squash. Pour syrup over the squash, letting it collect inside. Sprinkle with brown sugar. Pour about 2 ounces of water into the corner of each roasting pan. Cover the pans with foil. Bake for 60 minutes. Uncover and bake for 30 to 45 minutes longer or until a knife slides easily into the thickest part of the squash.

Uncover and cool for 15 minutes. Scoop the squash pulp into a large bowl; discard the skins. Drain the squash in a colander. Transfer to a bowl. Stir and serve. (The recipe can be prepared up to this point one day before serving, and then reheated in a casserole dish.)

Another serving idea is to spoon the squash into a baking dish. Bake, covered, at 350 degrees or until warm. Top with the goat cheese and bake for 5 minutes longer.

zucchini pie

2 tablespoons butter or margarine
4 cups sliced zucchini
1 cup chopped onion
2 tablespoons chopped parsley
1/2 teaspoon salt
1/2 teaspoon white pepper

1/4 teaspoon garlic powder
1/4 teaspoon oregano leaves
2 eggs, beaten
8 ounces mozzarella cheese
1 (8-count) can refrigerator crescent rolls
2 teaspoons Dijon mustard

Preheat the oven to 375 degrees. Melt the butter in a sauté pan and add the zucchini and onion. Sauté until tender. Stir in the parsley, salt, white pepper, garlic powder and oregano leaves. Combine the eggs and cheese in a bowl and mix well. Add to the vegetable mixture and mix well.

Separate the dough into eight triangles. Arrange in an ungreased baking pan. Press together to form a crust, pressing the dough up the sides of the pan. Spread the Dijon mustard over the dough. Pour the vegetable mixture into the prepared pan and spread evenly. Bake for 18 to 22 minutes or until a knife inserted into the center comes out clean. Let stand for 10 to 15 minutes before serving.

curried sweet potatoes

MAKES 6 TO 8 SERVINGS

4 large sweet potatoes
2 yellow onions

1/2 cup olive oil
Curry powder to taste

Preheat the oven to 375 degrees. Peel the sweet potatoes and cut into large cubes. Cut the onions into slices or strips. Arrange the sweet potatoes and onions in a 9x13-inch baking dish. Drizzle with the olive oil and toss to coat. Sprinkle generously with curry powder and toss to coat. Bake, uncovered, for 45 to 50 minutes or until cooked through.

creamy vegetable casserole

MAKES 6 SERVINGS

1 small head cauliflower, chopped
2 to 3 stalks broccoli, chopped
1 (4-ounce) can mushroom stems and pieces
1 (2-ounce) jar pimentos, drained
1 (6-ounce) can French-fried onions

1 cup (4 ounces) shredded Cheddar cheese
1 (10-ounce) can cream of mushroom soup
1/2 cup sour cream
Salt and pepper to taste

Preheat the oven to 325 degrees. Cook the cauliflower and broccoli briefly in boiling water in a saucepan. Plunge into cold water to stop the cooking process. Mix with the mushrooms in a bowl. Spoon into a baking dish. Mix the pimentos, half of the onions, half of the cheese, the soup, sour cream, salt and pepper in a bowl. Pour over the vegetables. Bake, covered, for 30 minutes. Uncover and top with the remaining cheese and onions. Bake for 5 minutes longer.

grilled corn and goat cheese-stuffed tomato

MAKES 4 SERVINGS

3 ears of corn, husks on
4 beefsteak tomatoes
1/2 cup sliced scallions
1/2 cup crumbled soft goat cheese

1 tablespoon white wine vinegar
1 tablespoon olive oil
Salt and freshly ground pepper to taste
3 bacon slices, crisp-cooked and crumbled

Pull back the corn husks, leaving them attached at the base. Remove the silks. Replace the husks. Cover the corn with water in a bowl. Let stand 10 minutes; drain. Cut off the top third of each tomato. Cut around the peel of each tomato to loosen the flesh. Squeeze out the seeds. Scoop out the tomato pulp, leaving a 1/4-inch shell. Chop the pulp and place in a bowl.

Preheat the grill to high. Place corn on lightly oiled grill racks. Grill, covered, for 15 to 20 minutes or until tender, turning occasionally. Remove from the grill. Pull back the husks and cut off the kernels. Add to the tomatoes. Add the scallions, all but 2 tablespoons of the goat cheese, the vinegar, 1 tablespoon olive oil, salt and pepper and mix well. Spoon into the tomato shells. Sprinkle with the remaining goat cheese and bacon.

chorizo and goat cheese stuffing

1 cup cooked chopped chorizo
6 tablespoons butter
1 large sweet onion such as Vidalia, finely chopped
3 tablespoons minced garlic
5 ribs celery, finely chopped
3 carrots, finely chopped

2 (16-ounce) packages plain or seasoned stuffing mix
1/4 cup fresh herbs (such as thyme, oregano or sage)
7 cups (about) low-sodium chicken stock
9 ounces goat cheese, crumbled
Salt and pepper to taste

Cook the chorizo in a large saucepan over medium heat until slightly crisp; drain. Do not wipe out or clean the pan. Melt the butter in the saucepan with the chorizo drippings and add the onion, garlic, celery and carrots. Sweat for about 5 minutes or until the onion is tender.

Preheat the oven to 350 degrees. Grease a 9x12-inch baking dish. Pour the stuffing into a large bowl. Add the chorizo and vegetables, including any pan juices and mix well. Add the herbs. Pour in the stock about 1 cup at a time until the stuffing mixture is very moist. Add the goat cheese and mix well. Season with salt and pepper. Spoon the stuffing mixture into the baking dish. Use a second greased baking dish if needed. Bake, uncovered, for 30 minutes or until stuffing is heated through and a golden brown crust has formed on top.

mushroom cognac risotto

1/4 cup (1/2 stick) butter
16 ounces fresh portobello mushrooms
2 shallots, minced
2/3 cup Cognac
3/4 cup heavy cream
2/3 cup Parmesan cheese

6 cups hot chicken stock
1 3/4 cups arborio rice
1/4 cup (1/2 stick) butter
Salt and pepper to taste
Chopped fresh chives for garnish

Melt the butter in a saucepan and add the mushrooms and shallots. Sauté until tender. Add the Cognac and simmer. Add the cream and cheese. Heat the butter in a saucpan and add the rice. Sauté briefly. Add 1/2 cup of the broth. Cook until the broth is absorbed, stirring constantly. Repeat with the remaining broth, cooking until the rice is creamy but grains are firm in the center. Garnish with chives.

cranberry and nut wild rice

MAKES 6 SERVINGS

1 cup dried cranberries
1/2 cup brandy
1 cup wild rice
2 cups chicken broth
1 cup orzo
2 cups chicken broth
1 fennel bulb, thinly sliced into 1-inch pieces

1 small red onion, chopped
3 tablespoons sherry vinegar
5 tablespoons walnut oil
2 teaspoons Dijon mustard
1/4 teaspoon freshly ground pepper
1/2 cup hazelnuts, chopped and toasted

Combine the cranberries and brandy in a small bowl and let stand. Cook the rice in a saucepan according to the package directions, using 2 cups broth. Remove from the heat and let stand to absorb any remaining broth. Cook the orzo in a saucepan according to the package directions, using 2 cups broth. Remove from the heat and let stand to absorb any remaining broth. Cool the rice and orzo. Combine the rice, orzo, cranberries, fennel and onion. Combine the vinegar, walnut oil, Dijon mustard and pepper in a bowl and whisk to blend. Add to the rice mixture and mix well. Add the hazelnuts and mix well. Chill in the refrigerator until serving time.

sweet and savory couscous

MAKES 4 TO 6 SERVINGS

1 tablespoon butter
1 small onion, chopped
1/4 cup raisins
1 1/2 cups chicken broth

1 (10-ounce) package plain couscous
1/4 cup slivered almonds
Salt and pepper to taste

Melt the butter in a saucepan and add the onion. Sauté until translucent. Add the raisins and broth. Bring to a boil. Stir in the couscous and almonds. Remove from the heat. Let stand, covered, for 5 to 10 minutes. Fluff with a fork. Season with salt and pepper.

butternut squash ravioli with sage and pine nuts

1 (10-ounce) package frozen butternut squash, thawed
2 tablespoons butter
3 ounces cream cheese, softened
2 teaspoons balsamic vinegar
2 tablespoons grated Parmesan cheese
1/4 teaspoon cinnamon

1/4 teaspoon nutmeg
Salt and pepper to taste
1 (12-ounce) package won ton wrappers
1/4 cup (1/2 stick) butter
12 fresh sage leaves
1/2 cup pine nuts
Parmesan cheese for garnish

Cook the squash in 2 tablespoons butter in a saucepan. Stir in the cream cheese. Add the vinegar, cheese, cinnamon, nutmeg, salt and pepper and mix well.

Lay one won ton wrapper on a work surface. Dip a pastry brush in water and brush all four edges of the wrapper. Place a spoonful of the squash mixture in the center. Top with a second won ton wrapper, pressing out as much air as possible. Repeat with the remaining wrappers and filling. (The ravioli may be frozen at this point.) Boil the ravioli in salted water for 2 to 3 minutes; drain. Spoon into a serving dish.

Melt 1/4 cup butter in a large sauté pan. Cook until it begins to brown. Add the sage and pine nuts. Pour over the ravioli. Garnish with cheese.

Won ton wrappers make it easy to prepare homemade ravioli. For larger ravioli, use egg roll wrappers and more filling.

poolside pesto pasta

4 cups loosely packed fresh basil leaves

5 garlic cloves, coarsely chopped

1 cup (4 ounces) freshly grated Parmesan cheese

1 cup extra-virgin olive oil

2 teaspoons salt

1/2 cup pine nuts

16 ounces penne

Salt and pepper to taste

Combine the basil, garlic, cheese, olive oil, salt and pine nuts in a blender or food processor. Process until thoroughly combined. Cook the pasta according to the package directions; drain. Toss with the pesto in a serving bowl. Season with salt and pepper. Serve immediately.

pasta caprese

MAKES 6 SERVINGS

16 ounces penne

10 Roma tomatoes

14 ounces fresh buffalo mozzarella cheese

3 garlic cloves

1 tablespoon salt

1/4 cup olive oil

3 tablespoons chopped basil

1/4 cup (1 ounce) freshly grated
Parmesan cheese

Cook the pasta according to the package directions; drain. Chop the tomatoes and mozzarella cheese. Mince the garlic. Combine the pasta with the tomatoes, mozzarella, garlic, salt, olive oil, and basil in a serving bowl and mix well. Top with the Parmesan cheese.

penne with rosemary cream sauce

MAKES 2 SERVINGS

8 ounces penne
1/4 cup rosemary, finely chopped
2 tablespoons olive oil
8 ounces puréed tomatoes

Salt and pepper to taste
2 ounces heavy cream
2 ounces grated Parmesan cheese

Cook the pasta in boiling salted water for 8 to 10 minutes or until al dente; drain. Sauté the rosemary in the olive oil in a saucepan over low heat for 3 minutes. Add the tomatoes, salt and pepper. Simmer for 15 minutes. Add the cream and cheese. Cook until heated through, stirring frequently. Toss with the pasta in a serving bowl.

white truffle macaroni and cheese

MAKES 10 TO 12 SERVINGS

5 cups cooked elbow macaroni
2 cups (8 ounces) shredded fontina cheese
2 cups (8 ounces) shredded asiago cheese
2 cups (8 ounces) shredded extra-sharp white
Cheddar cheese

1 teaspoon white pepper
1 teaspoon kosher salt
1 to 2 tablespoons white truffle oil
1 egg
1 cup milk

Preheat the oven to 350 degrees. Grease a 9x13-inch baking dish. Combine the fontina cheese, asiago cheese, Cheddar cheese and milk in the top of a double boiler over simmering water. Cook until the cheese is melted, stirring constantly. Add the salt and pepper. Add 1 tablespoon truffle oil for a subtle truffle taste, 2 tablespoons for a stronger presence. Let cool slightly.

Beat the egg in a small bowl. Add to the cheese mixture. Combine the cheese mixture with the macaroni in a bowl and mix well. Pour into the baking dish. Bake for 20 minutes.

desserts served

In addition to its commitment to delivering unparalleled journalism, Sun-Sentinel Company is dedicated to serving the community through programs such as the Sun-Sentinel Children's Fund, News in Education, and Sun-Sentinel Diversity Venture Fund. Since its inception in 1999 the Sun-Sentinel Children's Fund has raised more than $30 million for local underprivileged youth.

piña colada cake

MAKES 8 TO 10 SERVINGS

Cake	Pineapple Coconut Frosting
1 (2-layer) package white or coconut cake mix	3³/4 (3-ounce) packages vanilla instant pudding mix
1/3 cup rum	3¹/2 cups milk
	1¹/2 teaspoons coconut extract
	1 (20-ounce) can crushed pineapple, drained and juice reserved
	8 ounces cream cheese, softened
	16 ounces frozen whipped topping
	2 cups flaked coconut, toasted

For the cake, prepare the cake using the package directions, substituting the rum for a portion of the liquid. Bake in two greased and floured pans as directed. Cool completely.

For the frosting, combine the pudding mix, milk, coconut extract and reserved pineapple juice in a large mixing bowl. Beat for 2 minutes. Add the cream cheese and beat. Fold in the pineapple. Spread the frosting between the layers and over the top and side of the cake. Spread with a layer of whipped topping. Top with the toasted coconut.

Photo, page 130: *Piña Colada Cake, recipe this page*

chocolate turtle cake

1 (2-layer) package chocolate cake mix
1/2 cup (1 stick) butter
1 (14-ounce) package caramel
squares, unwrapped
1 (14-ounce) can sweetened condensed milk

1/2 cup coarsely chopped pecans
1/2 cup (1 stick) butter
2 cups (12 ounces) semisweet chocolate chips
1 1/2 cups coarsely chopped pecans

Preheat the oven to 350 degrees. Prepare the cake batter according to the package directions. Pour half of the batter into a very well-greased springform pan. Bake for 20 minutes. Melt 1/2 cup butter and the caramels in a saucepan over low heat. Remove from the heat. Add the condensed milk and mix well. Measure 3/4 cup of the mixture; set aside.

Pour 1/2 cup pecans around the perimeter of the cake where it has pulled away from the side of the pan. Pour the caramel mixture over the cake slowly. Pour the remaining cake batter over the caramel. Return to the oven for 30 to 35 minutes. Cool in the pan for 10 minutes. Remove from the pan.

Melt 1/2 cup butter with the chocolate chips in a saucepan over low heat. Pour the chocolate mixture over the cake, allowing it to drip over the side. Drizzle the top with the reserved 3/4 cup caramel mixture. Spread 1 1/2 cups pecans over the cake.

chocolate chip bundt cake

1 (2-layer) package butter-recipe cake mix
1 cup vegetable oil
1/4 cup water
1 (3-ounce) package chocolate instant
pudding mix

4 eggs
1 teaspoon vanilla extract
1 cup sour cream
1 cup (6 ounces) chocolate chips

Preheat the oven to 325 degrees. Combine the cake mix, oil, water, pudding mix, eggs, vanilla and sour cream in a bowl and mix well. Fold in the chocolate chips. Spoon the batter into a greased and floured bundt pan. Bake for 50 to 60 minutes; do not overbake. If a wooden pick inserted in the cake comes out clean, it is overbaked.

five-flavor pound cake

MAKES 12 TO 24 SERVINGS

1 cup (2 sticks) butter, softened	1 teaspoon coconut extract
1/2 cup shortening	1 teaspoon vanilla extract
3 cups sugar	1 teaspoon rum extract
5 eggs	1 teaspoon lemon extract
3 1/4 cups cake flour	1/2 cup sugar
1/2 teaspoon salt	1/3 cup water
1/2 teaspoon baking powder	1/2 teaspoon almond extract
1 cup milk	

Preheat the oven to 325 degrees. Beat the butter, shortening and 3 cups sugar in a bowl until smooth. Add the eggs one at a time, beating well after each addition. Combine the flour, salt and baking powder in a bowl. Add to the batter alternately with the milk, beginning and ending with the flour mixture, and mixing well after each addition. Fold in the flavorings, being careful not to overbeat. Spoon the batter into a greased and floured tube pan or bundt pan, or two greased and floured loaf pans. Bake for 1 1/2 hours (less for loaf pans) or until a wooden pick inserted in the cake comes out clean. Cool in the pan for 10 minutes. Combine 1/2 cup sugar and the water in a microwave-safe bowl. Microwave until the mixture comes to a boil. Stir in the almond extract. Invert the cake onto a serving platter. Drizzle with warm glaze.

red velvet cake

MAKES 16 SERVINGS

Cake

2 (1-ounce) bottles red food coloring
3 tablespoons baking cocoa
1/2 cup shortening
1 1/2 cups sugar
2 eggs, well beaten
2 1/2 cups cake flour
1 1/2 teaspoons baking powder
1/2 teaspoon baking soda
Pinch of salt
1 cup buttermilk
1 teaspoon vanilla extract

Creamy Frosting

1/2 cup (1 stick) margarine
1/2 cup shortening
1 cup sugar
3 tablespoons all-purpose flour
2/3 cup milk, at room temperature
2 teaspoons vanilla extract

For the cake, preheat the oven to 350 degrees. Combine the food coloring and the baking cocoa in a small bowl to form a paste; set aside.

Beat the shortening and sugar. Add the eggs and beat until well combined. Add the food coloring paste and mix well.

Combine the flour, baking powder, baking soda and salt in a bowl. Add the flour mixture to the batter alternately with the buttermilk and vanilla. Spoon into two greased 9-inch cake pans. Bake for 35 minutes. Cool in the pans for 10 minutes. Remove to a wire rack to cool completely.

For the frosting, beat the margarine, shortening and sugar. Add the flour 1 tablespoon at a time. Add the milk and vanilla. Beat until creamy. Spread the frosting between the layers and over the top and side of the cooled cake.

simply delicious chocolate cake

Cake

2 cups sugar
1 3/4 cups all-purpose flour
1 1/2 teaspoons baking soda
1 1/2 teaspoons baking powder
1 teaspoon salt
3/4 cup baking cocoa
2 eggs
1 cup milk
1/2 cup vegetable oil
2 teaspoons vanilla extract
1 cup boiling water

Fudgy Frosting

1/2 cup (1 stick) unsalted butter, melted
2/3 cup baking cocoa
1/3 cup milk
3 1/2 cups (about) confectioners' sugar
1 teaspoon vanilla extract

Preheat the oven to 350 degrees. Combine the sugar, flour, baking soda, baking powder, salt and baking cocoa in a bowl and mix well. Add the eggs, milk, oil and vanilla. Beat at medium speed for 2 minutes. Stir in the boiling water. Batter will be thin. Pour into two greased and floured 9-inch cake pans. Bake for 30 minutes or until cake springs back when lightly touched in the middle. Do not overbake. Cool in the pans for 10 minutes. Remove to wire racks to cool completely.

For the frosting, combine the butter and baking cocoa in a mixing bowl. Add the milk and confectioners' sugar alternately to make of a spreading consistency. Beat at medium speed. Beat in the vanilla. Spread the frosting between the layers and over the top and side of the cooled cake.

Prepare a double batch of the frosting for piping borders or adding designs.

P.S.

Alligators were named by early Spanish explorers, and the majority of all American alligators live in Florida and Louisiana. It is estimated that more than one million live in the Florida Everglades National Park in South Florida—the only place both alligators and crocodiles live side by side.

flourless chocolate espresso torte

MAKES 10 TO 12 SERVINGS

2 cups (4 sticks) unsalted butter	4 ounces bittersweet chocolate, chopped
1 cup sugar	8 ounces semisweet chocolate, finely chopped
1 cup brewed espresso	8 eggs, lightly beaten

Preheat the oven to 350 degrees. Combine the butter, sugar and espresso in a large saucepan and bring to a boil. Remove from heat and add the chocolates. Whisk until melted and well blended. Let cool slightly. Beat in the eggs with a whisk, but do not whip them.

Pour the mixture into a greased 12-inch springform pan lined with baking parchment. Place the springform pan into a larger baking pan. Place in the oven. Add enough water to the baking pan to reach 1 inch up the side of the springform pan. Bake for 30 minutes or until firm. Remove carefully. Let cool for 15 minutes. Chill in the refrigerator for 2 1/2 hours or until firm. Remove the torte from the pan. Cut with a warm knife.

If a 12-inch springform pan is not available, use a 10-inch springform pan and increase the baking time by 10 to 15 minutes.

chocolate toffee crunch cheesecake

1 3/4 cups crushed chocolate sandwich cookies

6 tablespoons butter, melted

1/4 cup sugar

32 ounces cream cheese, softened

2 teaspoons vanilla extract

4 eggs, lightly beaten

1 1/4 cups sugar

2 (8-ounce) packages toffee bits, 1/3 cup reserved

1/4 cup hot fudge topping

1/4 cup caramel topping

Preheat the oven to 350 degrees. Combine the cookie crumbs, butter and 1/4 cup sugar in a small bowl and mix well. Press the mixture over the bottom and 1/2-inch up the side of a 9-inch springform pan. Bake for 10 minutes. Let the crust cool slightly.

Beat the cream cheese in a large bowl until fluffy. Add the vanilla, eggs and 1 1/4 cups sugar and beat until creamy. Spoon half of the batter into the crust. Sprinkle with toffee bits to within 1 inch of the side. Top with the remaining cream cheese mixture, smoothing the top.

Bake for 45 to 55 minutes or until a wooden pick inserted in the center comes out clean. Prop open the oven door. Let the oven temperature drop gradually so the cake does not fall. The center should be a little soft when the cake is removed from the oven. Cool on a wire rack for 15 minutes. Release the springform pan side, and then reseal. Chill in the refrigerator for 8 hours or longer before slicing.

Slice and serve each piece topped with the hot fudge, caramel sauce and a sprinkling of the reserved toffee bits.

white chocolate mango cheesecake

MAKES 8 SERVINGS

1³/4 cups graham cracker crumbs

6 tablespoons butter, melted

¹/4 cup sugar

32 ounces cream cheese, softened

2 teaspoons vanilla extract

4 eggs, lightly beaten

1 cup sugar

1 cup (6 ounces) white chocolate chips, melted

14 ounces canned or thawed frozen mango
purée, or 1 (17-ounce) jar mango jam

¹/2 cup (3 ounces) white chocolate chips, melted

Preheat the oven to 350 degrees. Combine the graham cracker crumbs, butter and ¹/4 cup sugar in a small bowl and mix well. Press the mixture over the bottom and ¹/2 inch up the side of a 9-inch springform pan. Bake for 10 minutes. Let cool briefly.

Beat the cream cheese in a large bowl until fluffy. Add the vanilla, eggs and 1 cup sugar and mix until creamy. Add 1 cup white chocolate chips and mix well. Batter will be thick.

Spoon half of the batter into the springform pan. Drizzle all but ¹/4 cup of the mango purée over the batter to within 1 inch of the side. Top with the remaining batter, smoothing the top.

Spoon the reserved ¹/4 cup mango purée into a decorator bag fitted with a small writing tip. (Or use a sealable plastic bag and snip off the corner.) Pipe the purée in a zigzag pattern over the top of the batter. Repeat the motion in the opposite direction.

Bake for 45 to 55 minutes or until a wooden pick inserted in the center comes out clean. The center will be a little soft. Cool in the pan on a wire rack for 15 minutes. Release the springform pan side, and then reseal. Chill in the refrigerator for 8 hours or longer.

For the topping, spoon ¹/2 cup white chocolate chips into a decorator bag fitted with a tip. (Or use a sealable plastic bag and snip off the corner.) Pipe in a zigzag pattern over the top of the cheesecake.

sour cream cheesecake

MAKES 8 TO 10 SERVINGS

1 1/2 cups graham cracker crumbs or any cookie crumbs
3 tablespoons sugar
1/2 cup (1 stick) melted butter
1/2 teaspoon cinnamon
1/4 cup crushed walnuts (optional)

3 eggs
1 cup sugar
16 ounces cream cheese, softened
1/4 teaspoon salt
2 tablespoons vanilla extract
3 cups sour cream

Preheat the oven to 350 degrees. Combine the graham cracker crumbs, 3 tablespoons sugar, the butter, cinnamon and walnuts in a bowl and mix well. Press over the bottom of a 9-inch springform pan.

Beat the eggs, 1 cup sugar, the cream cheese, salt and vanilla in a mixing bowl until no small pieces of cream cheese are visible in the batter. Fold in the sour cream. Pour the batter into the prepared pan. Bake for 45 minutes. Turn off the oven. Prop open the oven door until the cheesecake is cool. Remove from the oven when completely cool.

For a twist, add baking cocoa and mint extract to the batter. Top with chocolate-covered peppermint patties.

double chocolate delight

MAKES 8 SERVINGS

1 1/2 cups chocolate wafer crumbs
1/3 cup melted butter
8 ounces cream cheese, softened
1/4 cup sugar
2 egg yolks
1 teaspoon vanilla extract

1 cup (6 ounces) semisweet chocolate chips, melted
3/4 cup chopped walnuts or pecans
2 egg whites
1/4 cup sugar
1 cup heavy whipping cream, whipped

Preheat the oven to 325 degrees. Combine the chocolate wafer crumbs and butter in a bowl. Press over the bottom of a 9-inch springform pan. Bake for 10 minutes. Let stand to cool.

Beat the cream cheese in a bowl until fluffy. Add 1/4 cup sugar, egg yolks, vanilla, melted chocolate and walnuts and mix well. Beat the egg whites with 1/4 cup sugar in a bowl until stiff peaks form. Fold into the chocolate mixture. Fold in the whipped cream. Pour into the crust. Freeze until firm.

If you are concerned about using raw eggs, substitute pasteurized eggs.

five-layer pudding dessert

1 cup all-purpose flour

1 cup finely chopped walnuts or pecans

1/2 cup (1 stick) butter or margarine, softened

8 ounces whipped topping

8 ounces cream cheese, softened

1 cup confectioners' sugar

2 (6-ounce) packages instant pudding mix, any flavor

3 cups 2 percent or whole milk

8 ounces whipped topping

Baking cocoa or shaved chocolate for garnish

Preheat the oven to 350 degrees. Combine the flour, walnuts and butter in a bowl and mix well. Press over the bottom of a 9x13-inch baking dish. Bake for 10 minutes or until light brown. Cool.

Beat 8 ounces whipped topping, the cream cheese and confectioners' sugar in a bowl until well blended. Spread over the cooled crust.

Beat the pudding mix with the milk in a bowl until thickened. Spoon over the cream cheese layer. Spread 8 ounces whipped topping over the top. Sprinkle with baking cocoa or shaved chocolate.

cherry yum yum

8 ounces cream cheese, softened

3/4 cup milk

1 cup confectioners' sugar

12 ounces whipped topping

1 large angel food cake

1 (20-ounce) can cherry pie filling

Combine the cream cheese, milk and sugar in the bowl of an electric mixer or with a hand mixer. Fold in the whipped topping.

Tear the cake into small pieces and place in a serving dish. Pour the cream cheese mixture over the cake layer. Spoon the pie filling over the cream cheese mixture. Chill in the refrigerator for at least 4 hours before serving.

old-fashioned baked custard

2 eggs, slightly beaten　　1 teaspoon vanilla
1 cup evaporated milk　　Few grains of salt
2/3 cup water　　Nutmeg to taste
1/2 cup sugar

Preheat the oven to 350 degrees. Combine the eggs, evaporated milk, water, sugar, vanilla and salt in a bowl and mix well. Pour into four custard cups. Sprinkle each with nutmeg. Place the cups in a baking dish. Add water to the baking dish to a depth of 1 inch. Bake for 45 minutes or until a knife inserted in the custard near the edge comes out clean. Let cool and then chill in the refrigerator. Serve cold or warm.

flan

MAKES 10 TO 12 SERVINGS

5 egg whites　　1 (14-ounce) can sweetened condensed milk
1 egg　　3 ounces cream cheese, softened
1 (12-ounce) can evaporated milk　　1/2 (1-pound) package sugar

Preheat the oven to 350 degrees. Combine the egg white, egg, evaporated milk, sweetened condensed milk and cream cheese in a blender. Process until smooth.

Heat a small nonstick skillet over high heat. Pour in the sugar. Cook until the sugar begins to turn light brown around the top edge, stirring constantly with a wooden spoon. Reduce the heat to medium-low. Cook until all the mixture has turned to caramel and the lumps are liquefied, stirring constantly. This happens quickly so remove the pan from the heat immediately when all the mixture is golden brown.

Pour the caramel evenly into two 6-inch pans. Tilt the pans to coat the sides. Process the egg mixture in the blender once more. Pour evenly into the pans. Cover the pans. Place in a large shallow pan filled halfway with water. Bake for 35 minutes or until a wooden pick inserted in the center comes out clean. Cool in the pans. Refrigerate for at least 1 hour. Invert the pans onto serving plates. Allow the caramel to drip onto the flan.

bananas foster

1/2 cup packed dark brown sugar	1/3 cup coconut rum or dark rum
2 tablespoons butter	Vanilla ice cream
6 ripe bananas, cut into halves lengthwise	

Combine the brown sugar and butter in a large skillet over medium heat. Cook until the butter melts and the sugar dissolves, stirring constantly. Add the bananas and turn to coat. Do not overcook the bananas.

Add the rum. Stand back and use a long match to ignite the alcohol. Let the flames subside. Spoon the bananas and sauce over ice cream in serving bowls. Serve immediately.

caramel fruit dip

MAKES 16 SERVINGS

10 Granny Smith apples, cored and sliced	1 teaspoon vanilla extract
1 (46-ounce) can pineapple juice	1 (15-ounce) jar caramel sauce
16 ounces cream cheese, softened	1/2 cup chopped walnuts
2 cups confectioners' sugar	

Soak the apples in the pineapple juice for 1 to 2 hours; drain and pat dry. Beat the cream cheese, confectioners' sugar and vanilla in a bowl until well combined. Spoon into a serving dish. Top with the caramel sauce. Sprinkle with the walnuts. Serve the apples with the dip.

grilled sugar-dipped pineapple

MAKES 6 SERVINGS

1 ripe pineapple	2 teaspoons cinnamon
1/2 cup (1 stick) unsalted butter	1/4 teaspoon ground cloves
1 1/2 cups sugar	1/2 dark rum (optional)
2 teaspoon grated lime zest	

Preheat the grill to high. Oil the grates. Peel the pineapple and cut out the eyes. Cut into eight to ten even rounds with a pineapple corer or sharp knife.

Melt the butter in a shallow bowl. Combine the sugar, lime zest, cinnamon and cloves in another bowl. Bring both bowls to the grill. Dip each slice of pineapple into the butter. Coat with the sugar mixture, shaking off any excess. Grill the pineapple for about 5 minutes per side, turning gently with tongs. Remove to a platter.

To flambé the pineapple, heat the rum briefly in a small saucepan set on the grill. Don't let it become hot. Remove it from the heat. Stand back and use a long match to ignite the rum. Pour the rum over the pineapple. Serve immediately.

strawberry pretzel dessert

1 (6-ounce) package strawberry gelatin mix
2 cups boiling water
3 cups sliced strawberries, chilled
3/4 cup (1 1/2 sticks) butter or margarine
3 tablespoons brown sugar

2 1/2 cups crushed pretzels
8 ounces cream cheese, softened
1 cup sugar
8 ounces whipped topping

Combine the gelatin with 2 cups boiling water in a large heatproof bowl. Add the strawberries. Chill in the refrigerator until the gelatin begins to set.

Preheat the oven to 350 degrees. Beat the butter and brown sugar in a bowl. Add the pretzels and mix well. Press over the bottom of a buttered 9x13-inch baking pan. Bake for 10 minutes. Cool.

Beat the cream cheese with the sugar. Fold in the whipped topping. Spread the cream cheese mixture over the cooled pretzel crust. Pour the gelatin mixture over the cream cheese layer. Chill in the refrigerator until firm. Cut into squares to serve.

Chef Greg Schramm has been cooking since age 9, beginning by making dinner at home while his mother gave instructions over the phone. From his first job bussing tables and learning some prep work, he headed to Johnson & Wales University right out of high school and straight for JM Family's Gallant Lady Yacht.

mile-high apple pie

MAKES 8 SERVINGS

Buttery Pie Pastry
1 1/2 cups all-purpose flour
2 tablespoons sugar
3/4 teaspoon salt
1/2 cup (1 stick) butter
4 to 6 tablespoons ice water

Streusel Topping
1/4 cup (1/2 stick) butter, softened
1/4 cup packed brown sugar
1/4 cup all-purpose flour
1/4 teaspoon cinnamon
1/2 cup chopped walnuts

For the pastry, combine the flour, sugar, salt and butter in a large bowl with a pastry blender or in a food processor. Add 2 tablespoons of the ice water and toss with a fork or pulse until incorporated. Add enough of the remaining ice water 1 tablespoon at a time until the mixture begins to form a dough, tossing or pulsing to incorporate.

Working on a flat surface, smear the dough in three or four forward motions with the heel of your hand to slightly develop the gluten in the flour and make the dough easier to work with. Form the dough into a ball. Flatten on plastic wrap into a 1-inch disk. Enclose in the wrap. Chill in the refrigerator for 30 minutes.

For the topping, combine the butter, brown sugar, flour and cinnamon in a small bowl with your fingertips until the butter is evenly incorporated. Stir in the walnuts. Chill, covered, in the refrigerator.

(continued on the following page)

Filling	1/4 teaspoon nutmeg
3 pounds Granny Smith apples	1/2 cup raisins
1 cup sugar	1 tablespoon all-purpose flour
2 tablespoons fresh lemon juice	Milk
1 teaspoon cinnamon	Sugar

For the filling, peel and core the apples. Cut into 1/2-inch-thick wedges. Combine with 1 cup sugar, the lemon juice, cinnamon, nutmeg, raisins and flour in a bowl and toss to coat. Preheat the oven to 350 degrees.

To assemble the pie, roll the dough on a lightly floured surface to a 15-inch round about 1/8 inch thick. Fold into quarters for easier handling. Unfold the dough in a 10-inch deep-dish pie dish, easing to fit and letting the dough overhang the rim of the pie dish. Spoon the filling into the pastry. Fold the pastry overhang over the filling, leaving the center uncovered. Place the pie on the middle oven rack. Bake for 1 hour (it will not be fully cooked). Crumble the topping over the center of the pie, breaking up any large chunks. Brush the crust with milk and sprinkle with sugar. Bake 30 minutes longer or until crust is golden brown and the filling is bubbling. Cool on a rack. Serve warm or at room temperature.

This recipe is from the kitchen of Chef Greg Schramm.

paradise served

crispy chocolate chip ice cream pie

MAKES 8 SERVINGS

1 cup chocolate syrup	1/3 cup sour cream
1/2 cup (3 ounces) semisweet chocolate chips	1 quart chocolate chip ice cream, softened
2 1/2 cups crisp rice cereal	

Spray an 8-inch pie dish with nonstick cooking spray. Combine the chocolate syrup and chocolate chips in a small microwave-safe bowl. Microwave on High for 45 seconds. Stir until smooth. Reserve 1/4 cup of the chocolate mixture.

Combine the remaining chocolate mixture with the cereal in a medium bowl and mix well. Press the mixture over the bottom and up the side of the prepared pie dish. Freeze for 15 minutes or until firm.

Combine the reserved 1/4 cup chocolate mixture and the sour cream in a small bowl and mix well. Spread half of the ice cream in the crust. Drizzle with half of the sour cream mixture. Top with the remaining ice cream. Drizzle with the remaining sour cream mixture. Cover with foil. Freeze for 1 hour or until firm.

triple-chocolate macadamia tart

Rich Pie Pastry
1/4 cup all-purpose flour
1 tablespoon sugar
1/2 cup (1 stick) butter, cut into pieces
1 egg yolk
2 tablespoons ice water

Filling
2 eggs
1 cup sugar
3/4 cup (1 1/2 sticks) butter, melted and cooled
1/2 teaspoon salt
1/2 cup all-purpose flour
1 tablespoon chocolate liqueur
1/2 cup (3 ounces) semisweet
   chocolate chips
1/2 cup (3 ounces) white chocolate chips
10 ounces whole macadamia nuts

For the pastry, combine the flour and sugar in a food processor. Add the butter. Pulse for 30 seconds. Add the egg and water. Process until the dough forms a ball. Roll the pastry on a flat surface. Pat over the bottom of a tart pan with a removable bottom. Chill in the refrigerator for 30 minutes.

For the filling, preheat the oven to 400 degrees. Beat the eggs and sugar in a bowl. Whisk in the butter, salt, flour and chocolate liqueur. Stir in the chips. Pour into the chilled tart shell. Sprinkle the macadamia nuts over the top. Press them gently into the filling. Bake for 10 minutes. Reduce the temperature to 350 degrees and bake for 35 minutes longer. Allow to cool before slicing.

pretty in peach cobbler

1/4 cup granulated sugar	1/2 cup granulated sugar
1/4 cup packed brown sugar	1 1/2 teaspoons baking powder
1 tablespoon cornstarch	1/2 teaspoon salt
1/2 cup water	1/2 cup milk
3 cups peeled peach chunks	1/4 cup (1/2 stick) butter, softened
1 tablespoon lemon juice	1 tablespoon sugar
1 cup all-purpose flour	1/2 teaspoon nutmeg

Preheat the oven to 375 degrees. Combine 1/4 cup granulated sugar, the brown sugar, cornstarch and water in a saucepan and mix well. Cook over medium heat until thickened, stirring constantly.

Combine the peaches with the lemon juice in a bowl. Spoon into a 2-quart baking dish. Add the cornstarch mixture and stir to coat.

Sift together the flour, 1/2 cup granulated sugar, the baking powder and salt in a bowl. Add the milk and butter and beat until smooth. Spoon over the peaches. Sprinkle with 1 tablespoon sugar and the nutmeg. Bake for 40 to 45 minutes. Serve warm.

nutty blondies

MAKES 16 BARS

1/3 cup butter or margarine	1/2 teaspoon baking powder
1 cup packed dark brown sugar	1/8 teaspoon baking soda
1 egg, beaten	1/2 teaspoon salt
1 teaspoon vanilla extract	1/2 cup chopped nuts (optional)
1 cup sifted all-purpose flour	1/2 cup (3 ounces) chocolate chips, or less to taste

Preheat the oven to 350 degrees. Melt the butter in a medium saucepan. Add the brown sugar and mix well. Add the egg and vanilla and mix well. Add the flour, baking powder, baking soda and salt and mix well. Stir in the nuts. Spoon the mixture into a greased 8-inch baking pan. Bake for 20 minutes. Cool in the pan.

beach blonde bars

MAKES 36 BARS

1 (2-layer) package butter cake mix
1 egg
1/2 cup (1 stick) butter, melted

3 eggs
8 ounces cream cheese, softened
1 (1-pound) package confectioners' sugar

Preheat the oven to 325 degrees. Combine the cake mix, egg and butter in a bowl. Press into a greased 9x13-inch baking pan. Beat the eggs with the cream cheese and confectioners' sugar in a bowl until well blended. Spoon over the cake layer. Bake for 1 hour. Cut into bars.

chippy dippy bars

1/2 cup (1 stick) butter
14 graham crackers
1 cup shredded coconut
1 cup (6 ounces) semisweet chocolate chips

1 cup (6 ounces) butterscotch chips or peanut
    butter chips
1 cup chopped walnuts
1 (14-ounce) can sweetened condensed milk

Preheat the oven to 325 degrees. Melt the butter in a medium saucepan. Crush the crackers to crumbs. Add to the butter and toss to coat. Press over the bottom of a 9x13-inch baking pan. Sprinkle with the coconut, chocolate chips, butterscotch chips and walnuts in the order listed. Pour the sweetened condensed milk evenly over the top. Bake for 25 minutes. Cut into bars.

coconut toffee macadamia cookies

MAKES 60 COOKIES

1 cup (2 sticks) butter, softened
1 cup packed light brown sugar
1/2 cup granulated sugar
1 egg
2 cups all-purpose flour

1 teaspoon baking soda
1 (14-ounce) package sweetened flaked coconut
6 ounces chopped macadamia nuts
1 (8-ounce) bag toffee chips

Preheat the oven to 375 degrees. Beat the butter, brown sugar, granulated sugar and egg in a bowl until well blended. Add the flour and baking soda and beat at low speed. Add the coconut, macadamia nuts and toffee chips and beat at high speed until well blended. The dough will be very stiff.

Roll heaping teaspoonfuls of the dough into balls. Flatten slightly between your palms. They should be around 2 1/2 inches across. Arrange on a cookie sheet. Bake for 10 to 12 minutes or until light brown. Cool for 2 to 3 minutes on the baking sheet, then remove promptly. Waiting longer may result in sticking. Cool completely.

forgotten cookies

2 egg whites
2/3 cup sugar
1 teaspoon vanilla extract

1/2 cup pecan pieces
1 cup (6 ounces) chocolate chips

Preheat the oven to 350 degrees. Beat the egg whites in a bowl using an electric mixer until firm peaks form. Beat in the sugar gradually. Stir in the vanilla, pecans and chocolate chips. Drop by teaspoonfuls onto greased baking sheets. Place in the oven. Turn off the oven. Leave the cookies in the oven for 6 to 12 hours; do not open the oven door.

gold rush brownies

MAKES 16 BARS

1 (15-ounce) box graham cracker crumbs
2 (14-ounce) cans sweetened condensed milk
2 cups (12 ounces) chocolate chips

1 cup walnuts (optional)
1/2 cup shredded coconut (optional)

Preheat the oven to 350 degrees. Combine all of the ingredients in a large bowl. Spread in a 9-inch baking pan sprayed with nonstick cooking spray. Bake for 35 to 40 minutes or until set.

no-bake chocolate cookies

MAKES 24 COOKIES

4 cups sugar
3/4 cup baking cocoa
1 cup milk
1/2 cup (1 stick) butter

1 cup peanut butter
1 teaspoon vanilla extract
6 cups quick-cooking oats

Combine the sugar, baking cocoa, milk and butter in a saucepan. Bring to a rolling boil for 1 minute, stirring frequently. Remove from the heat. Add the peanut butter, vanilla and oats, stirring to coat. Drop by tablespoonfuls onto baking sheets covered with waxed paper. Work quickly, as the mixture becomes more difficult to work with as it hardens.

neopolitas

1 (12-ounce) can almond pastry filling
1 cup (2 sticks) butter, softened
1 cup sugar
4 egg yolks
2 cups sifted all-purpose flour
4 egg whites
1/2 teaspoon red food
coloring (about 20 drops)

1/2 teaspoon yellow food
coloring (about 20 drops)
1/2 teaspoon green food
coloring (about 20 drops)
1/4 cup seedless red raspberry jam
1/4 cup apricot preserves
1 cup (6 ounces) semisweet chocolate chips

Preheat the oven to 350 degrees. Grease the bottom of three 9x13-inch pans. Line with waxed paper. Combine the almond filling, butter, sugar and egg yolks in a bowl. Beat at medium speed until light and fluffy. Stir in the flour with a wooden spoon.

Beat the egg whites until soft peaks form. Fold into the almond mixture. Measure out 1 1/2 cups and add the red food coloring. Spread the batter evenly in one of the prepared pans. Repeat the process with the remaining batter and food coloring. Bake the cakes for 10 to 15 minutes or until the edges are golden brown. Cool in the pan 10 minutes. Invert onto wire racks, turn cakes right side up, and cool completely.

Spread the raspberry jam evenly over the green layer. Top with the yellow layer. Spread the apricot preserves over the yellow layer. Top with the pink layer. Cover the top with plastic wrap. Set a heavy cutting board on the cake to weigh it down. Chill in the refrigerator for 8 hours or longer.

Melt the chocolate chips in a small saucepan set in a larger pan of hot water (or use a double boiler). Spread the melted chocolate over the cake. Trim the edges with a sharp knife. Let the frosting firm up for 15 minutes or until slightly dry.

Cut the cake crosswise into strips. Cut each strip into pieces.

The cakes get better over time, so consider making and frosting the cakes at least one day before serving. They're crowd pleasers, so make extra and freeze after cutting. Allow one hour for them to thaw.

brownies in a jar

MAKES 12 BARS

1 cup all-purpose flour
1/2 teaspoon salt
6 tablespoons baking cocoa
3/4 cup granulated sugar
1/2 cup packed brown sugar
3/4 cup granulated sugar
6 tablespoons baking cocoa

1/4 cup white chocolate chips
1/4 cup dark chocolate chips
1/4 walnuts
1/2 cup (1 stick) butter, melted
3 eggs
1/2 teaspoon vanilla extract

Combine the flour and salt. Pour into a 1-quart canning jar. Layer in 6 tablespoons baking cocoa, 3/4 cup granulated sugar, the brown sugar, 3/4 cup granulated sugar, 6 tablespoons baking cocoa and the chips in the order listed. Close the lid. Attach the walnuts to the jar.

Preheat the oven to 350 degrees. Pour the brownie mix into a bowl. Whisk to combine the ingredients. Stir in the butter, eggs and vanilla and mix well. Spread in a greased 9-inch baking pan. Bake for 35 minutes.

This brownie mix makes the perfect hostess or teacher gift. Tie a ribbon around the jar lid and attach the preparation directions.

chocolate peanut butter bars

MAKES 24 BARS

18 ounces chunky peanut butter
1 cup (2 sticks) butter, melted
1 (1-pound) package confectioners' sugar

1 1/2 cups graham cracker crumbs
1/2 cup (1 stick) butter
2 cups (12 ounces) chocolate chips

Combine the peanut butter, 1 cup butter, the confectioners' sugar and the cracker crumbs in a bowl. Mix by hand. Press into an ungreased 9x13-inch baking pan. Melt 1/2 cup butter in a saucepan with the chocolate chips. Pour over the peanut butter layer. Chill in the refrigerator for 30 minutes. Cut into bars.

crisp lemon thins

1/2 cup (1 stick) butter
3/4 cup packed light brown sugar
1 egg
3/4 cup all-purpose flour

1/2 cup blanched almonds, finely chopped
1/4 cup quick-cooking oats
1 tablespoon grated lemon zest
1/2 teaspoon lemon extract

Preheat the oven 350 degrees. Beat the butter and brown sugar in a bowl until light and fluffy. Add the egg and beat well. Beat in the flour, almonds, oats, lemon zest and extract and mix well. Drop by scant teaspoonfuls at least 3 inches apart on a greased baking sheet. Bake for 7 to 9 minutes or until the edges are golden brown. Remove and cool.

key lime bites

MAKES 48 TO 60 COOKIES

3/4 cup (1 1/2 sticks) softened butter
3/4 cup confectioners' sugar
2 tablespoons key lime juice
Zest of 2 limes
1 tablespoon vanilla extract

1 3/4 cups plus 2 tablespoons all-purpose flour
2 tablespoon cornstarch
1/2 teaspoon salt
1/4 cup confectioners' sugar

Beat the butter and 3/4 cup confectioners' sugar in a bowl until fluffy. Add the lime juice, lime zest and vanilla and mix well. Sift the flour, cornstarch and salt together. Add to the butter mixture and stir to combine. Roll the dough into two or three logs. Chill, wrapped in plastic wrap, in the refrigerator for 1 hour.

Preheat the oven to 350 degrees. Line a baking sheet with baking parchment. Slice the logs into 1/2-inch-thick rounds. Arrange on the the prepared baking sheet. Bake for 8 to 10 minutes or until slightly golden brown. Pour 1/4 cup confectioners' sugar in a sealable plastic bag. Remove the cookies from the oven; cool for 5 minutes. Add the cookies to the bag of confectioners' sugar. Shake to coat.

south florida celebrations served

sponsor
PUBLIX SUPER MARKETS CHARITIES

spring menu

can't passover this brisket
devil's in the details eggs
sweet kugel
homemade irish cream liqueur
spring has sprung cupcakes
guinness cupcakes

summer menu

paradise turkey burgers with mango salsa
sweet potato chips
caribbean pasta salad
french potato salad
crunchy coleslaw
festive fruit salad
light strawberry trifle
grilled peaches and caramel sauce

fall menu

apricot brandy turkey medallions
cranberry casserole
cuban thanksgiving stuffing
cranberry mandarin gelatin
squash soufflé
sweet potato casserole
butternut squash cheesecake with orange cranberry relish
pumpkin ice cream pie
perfect pumpkin pie

winter menu

twisted cherry meat loaf
'twas the night before casserole
potato latkes
ginger spice cookies
white walnut sugar cookies

can't passover this brisket

2 onions, sliced
2 tomatoes, chopped
1 flat-cut brisket
2 garlic cloves, pressed
1 envelope onion soup mix

1 teaspoon seasoned salt
1/2 cup water
1/2 cup white wine
1 tablespoon Worcestershire sauce
1/4 cup ketchup

Preheat the oven to 425 degrees. Combine the onions and tomatoes in the bottom of a foil roasting pan. Arrange the brisket flat side up over the vegetables. Rub the brisket with the garlic. Top with the onion soup mix, seasoned salt, water, wine, Worcestershire sauce and ketchup. Cover the pan with foil. Roast for 45 minutes. Reduce the temperature to 400 degrees. Baste the brisket with the pan juices. Roast for 30 minutes longer. Cool and then cut into thin slices at an angle.

devil's in the details eggs

8 eggs
2 tablespoons mayonnaise
2 tablespoons horseradish
1 teaspoon Dijon mustard

1/4 teaspoon dill weed
Salt and pepper to taste
Fresh dill weed

Combine the eggs with water to cover in a large saucepan. Bring to a boil over high heat. Cover the pot and turn off the heat, leaving the pot on the burner. Let stand for 15 minutes; drain. Refrigerate the eggs. Peel the eggs and then cut into halves lengthwise. Scoop the yolks into a bowl. Wipe any yolk residue from the whites. Arrange the whites on a plate.

Combine the yolks with the mayonnaise, horseradish, Dijon mustard, 1/4 teaspoon dill weed, the salt and pepper. Mix until creamy and smooth. Spoon into a pastry bag or a sealable plastic bag with one small corner snipped off. Pipe the yolk mixture into the whites. Garnish with fresh dill weed. Serve chilled.

Photo, page 158: Paradise Turkey Burgers with Mango Salsa, recipe page 166; French Potato Salad, recipe page 168; Sweet Potato Chips, recipe page 167

sweet kugel

MAKES 12 SERVINGS

1 pound wide egg noodles	6 eggs, beaten
2 cups sugar	4 cups whole milk
16 ounces small curd cottage cheese	1 teaspoon cinnamon
1/4 cup butter, softened	2 teaspoons vanilla extract
8 ounces cream cheese, softened	4 (single-serving) packages cornflakes, crushed

Preheat the oven to 350 degrees. Cook the noodles according to the package directions; drain. Combine with the sugar, cottage cheese, butter, cream cheese, eggs, milk, cinnamon and vanilla. Spoon into a greased 11x15-inch baking dish. Top with the cornflake crumbs. Bake, uncovered, for 90 minutes.

homemade irish cream liqueur

MAKES 10 SERVINGS

1 3/4 cups Irish whiskey	2 tablespoons chocolate syrup
1 (14-ounce) can sweetened condensed milk	2 teaspoons instant coffee granules
1 cup whipping cream	1 teaspoon vanilla extract
4 eggs	1/2 teaspoon almond extract

Combine the whiskey, sweetened condensed milk, cream, eggs, chocolate syrup, coffee granules and flavorings in a blender. Blend until well combined. Pour into a bottle and store, covered, in the refrigerator for up to 1 month. Stir before serving

If you are concerned about using raw egg, use eggs pasteurized in their shells, which are sold at some specialty food stores, or use an equivalent amount of egg substitute.

P.S.

Publix Super Markets was founded by George Jenkins in 1930. As much as he loved the grocery business, his passion for giving was even greater. He created the now named Publix Super Markets Charities in 1966 with the highest standards of philanthropic involvement and has contributed more than $250 million to support the community.

spring has sprung cupcakes

MAKES 12 CUPCAKES

Cupcakes
1/2 cup (1 stick) butter, softened
1 cup sugar
3 tablespoons cream cheese, softened
2 egg whites
2 teaspoons vanilla extract
11/2 cups all-purpose flour
13/4 teaspoons baking powder
1/2 cup milk
2 tablespoons pink sprinkles
1/4 cup shredded coconut

Fluffy Frosting
1 (1-pound) package confectioners' sugar
1 cup shortening
1 teaspoon meringue powder
1 teaspoon cream of tartar
3/4 teaspoon salt
2 teaspoons vanilla extract
1/4 cup milk
Food coloring

For the cupcakes, preheat the oven to 350 degrees. Beat the butter, sugar and cream cheese together in a bowl. Beat in the eggs one at a time; stir in the vanilla. Combine the flour and baking powder. Add to the butter mixture. Stir in the milk until well blended. Fold in the sprinkles and coconut. Spoon the batter into paper-lined muffin cups. Bake for 20 to 25 minutes or until the cupcakes spring back when touched in the center. Let the cupcakes cool for 1 hour.

For the frosting, combine the confectioners' sugar, shortening, meringue powder, cream of tartar, salt, vanilla and milk in a large bowl. Beat at high speed for 7 to 10 minutes or until fluffy. Beat in food coloring. Spoon the frosting into a pastry bag fitted with a leaf tip. Pipe flower petals onto the cupcakes. Use a star tip to pipe a center for each flower.

guinness cupcakes

MAKES 24 CUPCAKES

1 cup (2 sticks) butter, softened
18 ounces Guinness Stout
1/2 teaspoon vanilla extract
2 cups all-purpose flour
2 cups granulated sugar
3/4 cup baking cocoa
1 teaspoon salt
1 1/4 teaspoons baking soda

3/4 cup sour cream
1/4 cup each vegetable oil and chocolate syrup
1 (5-ounce) package chocolate instant
    pudding mix
3 large eggs
1/4 cup semisweet chocolate chips
4 teaspoons espresso powder
4 cups confectioners' sugar

Preheat the oven to 350 degrees. Combine 1/2 cup of the butter, 12 ounces of the beer and the vanilla in a small saucepan over medium heat. Cook until the butter melts, stirring frequently. Pour into a mixing bowl. Let cool for 10 minutes. Combine the flour, granulated sugar, baking cocoa, salt and baking soda in a large bowl. Beat the dry ingredients into the beer mixture in two additions with an electric mixer set at medium speed. Beat in the sour cream, oil, chocolate syrup and pudding mix. Beat in the eggs one at a time. Fold in the chocolate chips. Pour into paper-lined muffin cups. Bake for 23 to 25 minutes or until the cupcakes test done. Remove the cupcakes from the pan. Cool completely.

Combine the remaining 6 ounces beer and the espresso powder in a saucepan. Bring to a boil. Reduce the heat and simmer until reduced by half. Strain through a coffee filter. Cool. Beat the confectioners' sugar and the remaining 1/2 cup butter in a large bowl. Beat in the cooled beer mixture until the frosting reaches the desired consistency. Ice the cupcakes to resemble a pint of Guinness Stout.

Mangoes, an exotic fruit with the taste of a peach and a pineapple, play a leading role in tropical South Florida cuisine. Mangoes were found in Southeast Asia more than seven thousand years ago. Mango groves require hot, dry periods to produce a good crop.

paradise turkey burgers with mango salsa

MAKES 4 SERVINGS

1 pound ground turkey	1/2 teaspoon red pepper flakes
1 egg, beaten	1 ripe mango
1/3 cup bread crumbs	1/2 tablespoon sugar
1 tablespoon low-sodium soy sauce	1/2 onion, finely chopped
1 (2-inch) piece fresh ginger, chopped	Cilantro to taste
1/2 teaspoon cayenne pepper	Red pepper flakes to taste
1 teaspoon onion powder	

Combine the turkey, eggs, bread crumbs, soy sauce, ginger, cayenne pepper, onion powder and pepper flakes in a bowl and mix well. Form into four patties. Grill for 3 to 5 minutes per side or until cooked through.

Chop the mango. Add the sugar and onion and mix well. Add cilantro and pepper flakes. Chill until serving time.

sweet potato chips

4 or 5 large sweet potatoes   Coarse salt to taste
1 quart peanut oil

Peel the potatoes. Cut to the desired thickness with a mandoline. Thinner slices yield a crispier chip. Heat the peanut oil in a deep stockpot over high heat.

Add the potato slices a few at a time, enough to form a layer, being careful not to overcrowd the pot. Cook for about 4 minutes or until golden brown; turn and cook for 4 minutes longer or until golden brown. An 8-inch Chinese strainer works well for turning and removing the slices.

Drain on paper towels. Season with salt.

caribbean pasta salad

MAKES 10 TO 12 SERVINGS

1 pound orzo   1 (16-ounce) package frozen kernel corn, thawed
Salt to taste   1/2 yellow bell pepper, chopped
Drizzle of olive oil   1/2 orange bell pepper, chopped
1 onion, chopped   1/2 red bell pepper, chopped
1 bunch cilantro, chopped   Pepper to taste
1 pint grape tomatoes, cut into halves   Juice of 2 lemons
1 (28-ounce) can black beans, rinsed and drained   Olive oil

Cook the orzo in lightly salted water in a large saucepan to al dente; do not overcook. Drizzle with olive oil to prevent sticking. Let the pasta cool. Add the onion, cilantro, tomatoes, beans, corn and bell peppers. Season with salt and pepper. Add the lemon juice and enough olive oil to lightly coat the ingredients. Mix to combine. Serve cold or at room temperature.

french potato salad

MAKES 12 SERVINGS

4 pounds small red or white potatoes
Salt to taste
1/2 cup dry vermouth
1 1/2 cups blended mayonnaise and sour cream
1/4 cup white wine vinegar
1 teaspoon celery seeds

1 tablespoon sugar
Pepper to taste
2 large cucumbers, seeded and coarsely chopped
2 red onions, coarsely chopped
1/2 cup flat-leaf parsley, coarsely chopped

Cook the potatoes in boiling salted water until tender; drain. Let stand until cool. Whisk together the blended mayonnaise, vinegar, celery seeds, sugar, salt and pepper. Cut the potatoes into bite-size pieces and place in a serving bowl. Pour the dressing over the potatoes. Add the cucumbers, onions and parsley. Toss to combine. Serve at room temperature.

crunchy coleslaw

1 (16-ounce) bag coleslaw mix
1 (3-ounce) package ramen noodles, crushed
8 scallions, sliced
1/2 cup sunflower seeds
1/2 cup sliced almonds

3/4 cup canola oil
6 tablespoons sugar
6 tablespoons white vinegar
2 tablespoons Accent seasoning
Salt and pepper to taste

Combine the coleslaw mix, ramen noodles, scallions, sunflower seeds and almonds in a large bowl and mix well. Combine the canola oil, sugar, vinegar, seasoning, salt and pepper in a small bowl and whisk to blend. Just before serving, pour the dressing over the salad and toss to combine.

festive fruit salad

MAKES 12 SERVINGS

3 egg yolks, well beaten
1/2 cup cream
1/4 cup lemon juice
1/8 teaspoon salt
1 (12-ounce) can cherries

1 (20-ounce) can pineapple chunks
1 1/2 cups blanched, slivered almonds
8 ounces miniature marshmallows
1 cup heavy whipping cream, whipped

Combine the egg yolks, cream, lemon juice and salt in a saucepan. Cook until thickened, stirring constantly. Let the dressing cool. Combine the cherries, pineapple, almonds and marshmallows in a large bowl. Add the dressing and fold to combine. Fold in the whipped cream. Chill in the refrigerator for 8 hours or longer.

A member of the rose family, the strawberry is named for the common practice of growing berries under straw to protect them from cold and frost. Today the strawberry is the leading small fruit crop in the United States and is farmed mainly in Florida and California.

light strawberry trifle

MAKES 8 SERVINGS

2 tablespoons sugar
3 pints strawberries, cut into halves
8 ounces fat-free cream cheese, softened
2 tablespoons sugar
16 ounces fat-free whipped topping

1 fat-free or light pound cake
3 tablespoons sherry
1 cup seedless raspberry jam
Whole strawberries

Sprinkle 2 tablespoons sugar over the strawberry halves in a bowl. Beat the cream cheese and 2 tablespoons sugar in a bowl. Fold in the whipped topping a small amount at a time.

Cut the cake into slices 1/3 inch thick. Arrange a layer of half the cake slices in a trifle bowl. Sprinkle with half the sherry. Melt the jam in a saucepan or microwave-safe dish. Spread over the cake layer. Layer with half the strawberry halves and half the cream cheese mixture. Repeat the layers, ending with cream cheese mixture. Garnish with whole strawberries.

grilled peaches and caramel sauce

Grilled Peaches
8 unpeeled ripe peaches, cut into halves
1/2 cup packed brown sugar
1/4 cup (1/2 stick) butter, melted

Caramel Sauce
1/2 cup (1 stick) butter
1/2 cup packed brown sugar
1/2 cup granulated sugar
1/2 cup whipping cream
1 teaspoon vanilla extract

Assembly
Vanilla ice cream

For the peaches, clean the grill well to prevent peaches from absorbing other flavors. Oil the grates. Grill the peaches cut side down over medium coals for 6 minutes. Turn the peaches and fill each hollow with 1 tablespoon of the brown sugar and 1/2 tablespoon of the butter. Grill for 3 minutes longer.

For the sauce, combine the butter, brown sugar, granulated and whipping cream in a heavy medium saucepan. Bring to a boil over medium heat, stirring frequently. Boil for 1 minute, stirring constantly. Cool slightly and stir in the vanilla. Slice the warm grilled peaches and serve with the ice cream. Drizzle with the caramel sauce.

The sauce can be stored, covered, in the refrigerator for up to 5 days. Warm before serving.

apricot brandy turkey medallions

MAKES 3 TO 6 SERVINGS

3 (8-ounce) boneless skinless turkey tenderloins
1/2 cup all-purpose flour
Salt and pepper to taste
3 tablespoons butter
1 tablespoon finely chopped shallot
2 pounds button mushrooms

1/2 cup apricot brandy
1 cup chicken stock, chilled
1 tablespoon cornstarch (optional)
1/4 cup cream
1/2 cup shaved Parmesan cheese
Chopped fresh Italian parsley

Place each turkey tenderloin on a cutting board. Remove the white tendon with a sharp knife. Cut each into halves. Place each piece of turkey between two layers of plastic wrap or waxed paper. Pound to an even thickness. Coat each with the flour, shaking off any excess. Season with salt and pepper.

Melt the butter in a 12-inch sauté pan and add the shallots. Sauté over medium heat until tender. Add the turkey, placing the more attractive side down first. Cook until golden brown; turn the turkey over and add the mushrooms. Pour the brandy over the turkey. Cook for 2 minutes or slightly reduced. Add the stock. If you like a thicker sauce, stir the cornstarch into the stock before adding. Move the ingredients around in the pan, bringing the tenderloins to the top, away from the heat, to allow the mushrooms to finish cooking. Add the cream. Simmer for 2 minutes or until sauce thickens to the desired consistency. Season with salt and pepper. Garnish with the cheese and parsley.

cranberry casserole

MAKES 6 TO 8 SERVINGS

3 cups chopped apples (4 or 5 apples)
1 cup fresh cranberries
1 1/4 cups sugar
1 1/2 cups granola cereal without raisins

1/3 cup flour
1/2 cup (1 stick) butter, melted
1/2 cup chopped pecans
1/2 cup packed brown sugar

Preheat the oven to 350 degrees. Combine the apples, cranberries and sugar in a bowl. Pour into a greased 9x12-inch glass baking dish. Combine the granola, flour, butter, pecans and brown sugar in a bowl and mix well. Spread over the apple mixture; it will not fully cover the fruit. Bake for 1 hour.

cuban thanksgiving stuffing

MAKES 8 SERVINGS

1 pound spicy bulk pork sausage
1 cup (2 sticks) butter
1 large onion, minced
4 garlic cloves, minced
Salt and pepper to taste
1 (16-ounce) package corn bread stuffing mix
2 teaspoons salt
2 teaspoons thyme

1 teaspoon nutmeg
2 cups heavy whipping cream
1 cup cooking sherry
2 (3-ounce) packages pecan pieces
1 (12-ounce) package orange-flavored seedless prunes or cranberries, cut into halves
3 Granny Smith apples, peeled, cored and chopped

Cook the sausage in a skillet on the stovetop or in the microwave until brown and crumbly; drain on paper towels. Melt the butter in a skillet over low heat. Add the onion and garlic. Sauté over low to medium heat or until tender. Season with salt and pepper to taste. Add the stuffing mix, 2 teaspoons salt, the thyme, nutmeg, cream, sherry, pecans, prunes and apples and mix well. Spoon the stuffing into a turkey and cook according to the roasting directions. Or, cook the stuffing in a baking dish in a 400-degree oven for 20 minutes.

cranberry mandarin gelatin

MAKES 10 SERVINGS

2 (6-ounce) packages raspberry or cranberry gelatin
4 cups hot water
2 cups cold water

2 (16-ounce) cans jellied cranberry sauce
Zest and juice of 2 lemons
2 (11-ounce) cans mandarin orange, drained

Prepare the gelatin according to the package directions using 4 cups hot water and 2 cups cold water. Add the cranberry sauce, using a potato masher to blend it in thoroughly. Add the lemon zest and juice and mix well. Chill in the refrigerator for 1 1/2 hours or until the mixture is thick enough to fold in the oranges. Fold in the oranges and pour into a 64-ounce gelatin mold. Refrigerate for 8 hours or longer.

squash soufflé

1 (12-ounce) package frozen squash, thawed
1/4 cup sugar
1/2 cup all-purpose flour
3 eggs
2 cups milk

1/4 cup (1/2 stick) butter, melted
Salt to taste
Cinnamon to taste
Nutmeg to taste

Preheat the oven to 350 degrees. Combine the squash and sugar in a bowl and mix well. Add the flour, eggs, milk, butter, salt, cinnamon and nutmeg and mix well. Spoon into a greased baking dish. Bake for 1 hour and 20 minutes or until a knife inserted into the soufflé comes out clean. The soufflé won't stay puffed for long, but it's still delicious after it falls.

sweet potato casserole

Sweet Potatoes
3 cups mashed cooked sweet potatoes
1/2 cup sugar
1/2 teaspoon salt
2 eggs, lightly beaten
1/3 stick butter, melted
1 teaspoon vanilla extract
1/2 cup milk

Pecan Topping
1/4 cup (1/2 stick) butter
1 cup packed brown sugar
1/3 cup all-purpose flour
1 cup chopped pecans

For the sweet potatoes, preheat the oven to 350 degrees. Combine the sweet potatoes, sugar, salt, eggs, butter, vanilla and milk in a bowl and mix well. Spoon or pour into a greased 2-quart baking dish.

For the pecan topping, melt the butter in a saucepan. Add the brown sugar, flour and pecans and cook over medium heat for 2 minutes. Spread over the sweet potatoes. Bake for 35 minutes.

butternut squash cheesecake with orange cranberry relish

Butternut Squash Cheesecake

1 large butternut squash, cut into halves and seeded

3 tablespoons butter, melted

1 1/2 cups vanilla wafer cookie crumbs

32 ounces cream cheese, softened

1 1/4 cups sugar

1 teaspoon vanilla extract

1/2 teaspoon ancho chili powder to taste

4 egg yolks

3 eggs

Orange Cranberry Relish

16 ounces cranberries

1 unpeeled navel orange, chopped

1 1/2 cups sugar

1 teaspoon vanilla extract, or 1/2 vanilla bean, scraped

1 cup coarsely chopped toasted nuts such as pecans, pistachios or walnuts (optional)

Zest of 1 lemon

For the cheesecake, preheat the oven to 400 degrees. Bake the squash in a baking pan for 45 minutes or until tender. Maintain the oven temperature. Scoop out the squash pulp in chunks. Let cool. (This step can be done 1 day in advance.)

Combine the butter and the cookie crumbs in a bowl and mix well. Press over the bottom of a 9-inch springform pan. Process the cream cheese and the sugar in a food processor fitted with a metal blade until well blended. Or, beat in an electric mixer fitted with a paddle attachment at high speed until well blended. Add the squash, vanilla and chili powder and mix until combined. Add the egg yolks and eggs one at a time, mixing thoroughly after each addition. Pour over the prepared crust. Bake for 20 minutes. Reduce the temperature to 325 degrees. Bake for 40 to 60 minutes longer or until the center no longer jiggles when the pan is shaken. Remove from the oven to a wire rack. Cool for 1 hour. Chill in the refrigerator until completely cooled. Remove the side of the pan.

For the relish, combine the cranberries, orange, sugar and vanilla in a food processor fitted with a metal blade. Pulse on and off to a chunky texture. Remove to a nonreactive bowl. Add the nuts and lemon zest and mix well.

This recipe is from the kitchen of Chef Chris Wilber.

pumpkin ice cream pie

1 pint French vanilla ice cream, softened	1 teaspoon cinnamon
1 (9-inch) graham cracker pie shell	1/2 teaspoon ginger
2 cups pumpkin purée	1/4 teaspoon ground cloves
1 1/2 cups sugar	1 teaspoon vanilla
1/2 teaspoon salt	1 cup whipped topping

Spread the ice cream over the bottom of the pie shell. Freeze until firm. Combine the pumpkin, sugar, salt, cinnamon, ginger, cloves and vanilla and mix well. Fold in the whipped topping. Spread the evenly over the ice cream. Freeze until firm.

perfect pumpkin pie

MAKES 6 TO 8 SERVINGS

Pie Pastry	Pumpkin Filling
2 cups all-purpose flour	2 eggs, beaten
1 teaspoon salt	1 cup sugar
2/3 cup shortening	1 (15-ounce) can pumpkin
5 to 6 tablespoons cold water	1 tablespoon all-purpose flour
	1 cup milk
	1/4 cup (1/2 stick) butter, melted
	1 teaspoon vanilla extract
	1/2 teaspoon ginger
	1 teaspoon cinnamon
	1 teaspoon nutmeg
	1/2 cup whiskey (optional)

For the pastry, combine the flour and salt in a bowl. Cut in the shortening with a pastry blender until the pieces are the size of small peas. Add the water by the teaspoonful, stirring with a fork until the mixture forms a ball. Place on a waxed paper square. Shape into a compact ball using waxed paper. Chill. Roll about 1/8 inch thick on a lightly floured surface. Fit into a 9-inch pie dish. Preheat the oven to 400 degrees.

For the filling, combine the eggs, sugar, pumpkin, flour, milk, butter, vanilla, ginger, cinnamon, nutmeg and whiskey in the order listed. Pour into the pie pastry. Bake for 10 minutes. Reduce the temperature to 325 degrees and bake for 45 minutes or until a knife inserted in the center comes out clean.

twisted cherry meat loaf

MAKES 4 TO 6 SERVINGS

Meat Loaf and Baste
1 pound smoked ham
8 ounces ground beef
1 egg, beaten
1/2 cup milk
1/2 cup dry bread crumbs
1 teaspoon finely chopped onion
Dash of salt
Dash of celery salt
1/2 cup packed brown sugar

1/2 tablespoon dry mustard
1/4 cup apple cider vinegar
1/4 cup water or pineapple juice

Cherry Sauce
1 (15-ounce) can pitted tart red cherries
1/2 cup sugar
2 tablespoons cornstarch
1/4 teaspoon ground cloves

For the meat loaf, preheat the oven to 350 degrees. Grind the ham and beef together in a food processor. Add the egg, milk, bread crumbs, onion, salt and celery salt and mix well in the food processor or with your hands. Pat the mixture into a loaf and place in a loaf pan or baking pan.

Mix the brown sugar, mustard, vinegar and water in a bowl. Baste the meat loaf. Bake the meat loaf for 1 1/2 to 2 hours or until cooked through, basting every 15 to 30 minutes with the brown sugar mixture.

For the cherry sauce, drain the cherries, reserving the liquid. Combine the cherry liquid, sugar, cornstarch and cloves in a saucepan and mix well. Cook until the mixture thickens, stirring constantly. Stir in the cherries. Simmer until heated through. Serve over the meat loaf.

paradise served

177

'twas the night before casserole

1 1/2 pounds bulk pork sausage
3 cups water
3/4 cup grits
4 cups (16 ounces) shredded sharp
Cheddar cheese

4 eggs
1 cup milk
1 teaspoon garlic powder

Preheat the oven to 350 degrees. Brown the sausage in a skillet, stirring until crumbly; drain. Bring the water to a boil in a saucepan. Stir in the grits. Reduce the heat to low and cook for 5 minutes. Add the cheese and cook until the cheese melts, stirring constantly.

Whisk the eggs, milk and garlic powder in a large bowl. Add the grits and mix well. Stir in the sausage. Pour into a 9x13-inch pan. Bake for 50 minutes. Serve or chill in the refrigerator. Reheat at 350 degrees for 25 minutes.

Many holidays have early-morning festivities. This recipe is ideal because it can be made in advance of time and gets even better in the refrigerator overnight. Just put it in the oven and enjoy more family time!

potato latkes

3 pounds baking potatoes
1 large yellow onion
2 eggs
1/4 cup all-purpose flour

1/2 teaspoon kosher salt
1/4 teaspoon pepper
Vegetable oil or peanut oil for frying

Peel and shred the potatoes on a box grater (do not use a food processor) into a colander over a large bowl. Grate the onions into the colander. Pour off the water but leave the starch that has collected in the bowl. Add the eggs, flour, salt, pepper and the reserved starch to the potatoes and mix well.

Heat 1/2 inch of oil in a large skillet. Drop 1/4 cupfuls of the potato mixture into the oil, leaving at least 1 inch between latkes. Brown for 3 to 5 minutes per side. Drain on paper towels.

Serve with sour cream or applesauce.

ginger spice cookies

2 cups all-purpose flour
2 teaspoons baking soda
2 teaspoons ginger
2 teaspoon cinnamon
2 teaspoons ground cloves
1 teaspoon salt

3/4 cup (1 1/2 sticks) butter, softened
1 cup packed light brown sugar
1 egg
1/4 cup molasses
2 teaspoons orange zest
1/2 cup granulated sugar

Combine the flour, baking soda, ginger, cinnamon, cloves and salt in a bowl. Beat the butter with the brown sugar in a bowl until fluffy. Beat in the egg, molasses and orange zest. Fold in the dry ingredients until just combined; do not overmix. Chill, covered, in the refrigerator.

Preheat the oven to 350 degrees. Roll the dough into 1 1/2-inch balls and coat the tops in the granulated sugar. Arrange on a nonstick cookie sheet. Bake for 12 minutes or until cracked on top but still soft. Cool on the sheet for 2 minutes. Remove to a wire rack to cool completely.

white walnut sugar cookies

MAKES 75 COOKIES

2 cups (4 sticks) butter, softened
1 (1-pound) package sugar
6 eggs
1 teaspoon vanilla extract
5 cups all-purpose flour

2 teaspoons baking powder
1/2 teaspoon salt
1 cup walnuts, finely chopped
Tinted sugars for decoration

Preheat the oven to 350 degrees. Beat the butter, 1 pound sugar and the eggs in a large bowl. Add the vanilla and mix well. Combine the flour, baking powder and salt in a bowl. Add to the butter mixture and mix well. Stir in the walnuts.

Roll the dough to a 1/4-inch thickness on a lightly floured surface. Cut out shapes with cookie cutters. Arrange the cookies on a nonstick baking sheet. Decorate with tinted sugars. Bake for 10 minutes. Cool completely.

cookbook development committee

Rochelle Darman and Lori Ebinger Sullivan
Co-Chairs

Candy Johnson
Sustaining Advisor

Active Members	*Provisional Members*
April L. Alder	Jacqueline Blake
Michelle Dowsett Black	Kandi Osman
Sheree Bonsett	Janice Sham
Michelle del Valle	Elizabeth Swann
Kimberly Jaeger	Sarah Templeton
Wendy Harrigan	
Nikol Johnson	
Suzanne Lang	
Lisa Malanowski	
Tracy Reese	
Christine Rickard	

Photo Caption: (L to R) Michelle Dowsett Black, Janice Sham, Kandi Osman, Christine Rickard, Lori Ebinger Sullivan, Sarah Templeton, Sheree Bonsett, Lisa Malanowski, Tracy Reese, Rochelle Darman, Jacqueline Blake, April L. Alder, Nikol Johnson, Suzanne Lang, Kimberly Jaeger, and Michelle del Valle. Not pictured: Wendy Harrigan, Candy Johnson, and Elizabeth Swann.

2007–2008 board of directors

Audrey Ring
President

Tara McGinn
President-Elect

Kate Lochrie
Community Vice President

Jennifer Ramach
Finance Vice President

Gina Ciolino Reynen
Marketing Vice President

Cindy Worden
Membership Vice President

Christine Von Wyl
Nominating

Alicia Malinowski
Parliamentarian

Dawn Huckestein
Provisional Education

Heather Moraitis
Provisional Education

Billie Dalglish
Recording Secretary

Barbara Keith
Sustaining Advisor

Kimberly Fundaro
Treasurer

acknowledgments

*The Cookbook Development Committee would like to acknowledge
and sincerely thank our families and friends who have lovingly supported
us this year as we worked together to produce* Paradise Served.

*The Committee also wishes to acknowledge the contribution of
time, talent, and support from these special individuals and companies:*

Deborah Dunn, Silpada Designs

Divers Direct

Deborah S. Hartz-Seeley

Magdalena Hernandez,
www.magdalenaphotography.com

Candy Johnson, The Cactus Flower

Junior League of Greater Fort Lauderdale's
2007–2008 Provisional Class

Publix Super Markets, Inc.

Gina Ciolino Reynen

Kevin and Shelley Senecal

Jessica Urbanski

Donald and Sheri Whittington

PUBLIX SUPER MARKETS
CHARITIES

Sun-Sentinel

recipe contributors

April L. Alder
Jeanne Alder
Wayne Alder
Nazira Ali
Annette Alvarez
Eliana Anderson
Rosemary "Rosie" Armstrong
Fran Arnold
Martha Barber
Dorothy Basgall
Councilwoman Diane
    Veltri Bendekovic
Stephanie Berman
Wendy Berman
Linda Bird
Jacqueline Blake
Marci Boland
Sheree Bonsett
Carolyn Bradley
Meagan Bradley
Barbara Breitling
Kathie Brennan
Doris A. Bricker
Paige Brody
Napoleon Bonaparte
    Broward Family
Kristin Byk
Jessica Carmen
Sandra Casteel
Hayes Chamoun
Carole E. Clifford
Tonja Haddad Coleman
Virginia Voet Coleman
Penny Cummings
Terry D'Alessandro
Billie Dalglish
James P. Dalglish
Rochelle Darman
Cherita Davis

Jessica DeBianchi
Michelle Delaplaine
Michelle del Valle
Ebony Diaz-Snell
Irma Doerfler
Todd Doerfler
Melissa Donalson
Susan Duff
Carolyn Dunn
Deborah Dunn
Shelley Dwinal
Margaret P. Egan
Melissa Erb
Angela Erskine
Liz Ferayorni
Deb Ferguson
Chef Carlos Fernandez
Chef Curt Fisher
Commissioner Pat Flury
Molly Fogel
Katie Foreman
Ethel Fullman
Reyanne Gailing
Susan Gallion
Mel Garraway
Janice Garter
Marilyn Gerber
John Gerbino
Mayor Larry Gierer
Gigi's
Allison Gilchrest
Julie Goel
Irma D. Gonzalez
Judge Jose A. Gonzalez, Jr.
Quinn Goodchild
Pura Gordon
Connie Granja
Liz Grant
Jaime Guillen

Commissioner Sue Gunzburger
Guy Harvey's Island Grill
Liz Hadgkiss
Wendy Harrigan
Congressman Alcee L. Hastings
Sharon Hatfield
Pam Heichel
Erin Hemminger
Diane Howard
Kiarra Howe
Michelle Hopkins
Coleen Hubbard
Dawn Huckestein
Tracy Huggins
Kristi Hurst
Jane Huston
Commissioner Cindi Hutchinson
Chef Cindy Hutson
Becky Irwin
Chef Robert Jacobs
Kim Jaeger
Jayne Jett
Tania Johansen
Nikol Johnson
Commissioner Sandy Johnson
Karen M. Jones
Rees Jones
Princesita Juvida
Joyce Kaiser
Mayor Richard J. Kaplan
Constanza Kehren
Barbara Keith
Billie Weil Kelly
Deborah Kerr
Patricia Kodish
Laura Kottke
Dawn Kravitz
Kristi Krueger

recipe contributors

Freida Kutch
Suzanne Lang
Susan Lawton
Gail Lewis
Jennifer Little-Kiss
Susan Lochrie
Gerry Loehr
Patricia Lucey
Jennifer Lucy
Chef Matthew Ludka
Diane Magary
Lisa Malanowski
Van Thomas Malinowski
Lisa Mallozzi
Margaret Martin
Nicholle Maudlin
Chef Dean Max
Amy McCarthy
Tara McGinn
Joey McIntyre
Martie Mehallis
Merrie Meyers-Kershaw
Diane Minutoli
Elizabeth Moffitt
Aagje Monteleone
Heather Moraitis
Michael Morales
Chad Moss
Maha Mourad
Kim A. Naimoli
Merle A. Naylon
Sandy Naylon
Senator Bill Nelson
Elaine Nemezio
Rhonda Lang Netzel
Kaye Newman
Denise Nicely
Sharon Palagi O'Donnell

John Ofciarcik
John Offerdahl
Christine O'Loughlin
Alexandra Moraitis Orman
Kandi Osman
Laura Overmyer
Karen Owen
Sue Perdomo
Jenny Perez
Michelle Perry
Lauren Presson
Angela Pohlman
Dorothy Porges
Thelma G. Portnoy
Bunny Ragland
Dana "Bunny" Riley
Tracy Reese
Andrea Rist
Gayle Roberts
Kate Rodriguez
Monique Rowan
Mary Lou Ruderman
David Ruiz
Sally Ruttger
Marilyn Sakowicz
Andy Sarkisian
Mildred Schlossberg
Congresswoman Debbie
    Wasserman Schultz
Holly Schnier
Chef Greg Schramm
Patti Scott
Sara Sears
Shelley Senecal
Rick Shaw
Joshua Shea
Aletta L. Shutes
Casey C. Simmons
Paula Skinner

Kevin Songer
Maria Spinaci
Paulette Spinks
Chef Daniel "Staz" Stasi
Kirsten Stephenson
Joe Stern
Gary Stern
Mary Stoudt
Lori Ebinger Sullivan
Marc L. Sultanof
Elizabeth Swann
Cheryl Tape
Linda Tapp
Sarah Templeton
Joan Tessmer
Terri Trent
Jessica Urbanski
JoAnn Vales
Laura Vance
Cheri Vancuras
Marlena M. Vareles
Ilene Vitkus
Rebecca Vitkus
Emma Jean Voet
Laura Voet
Lynde Voet
Christine Von Wyl
Julie Weil
Ellen Whiteman
Chef Chris Wilber
Daniel Wilkinson
Julie Wilkinson
Claudia Willey
Carol Witman
Cookie Zicaro
Judi Zito

recipe testers

Nicole Abelson
April L. Alder
Amanda Allen
Eliana Anderson
Christina Antimucci
Leslie Barber
Emily Bartkowicz
Gaye Bengochea
Patty Bilowich
Lisa Bisagni
Michelle Black
Jacqueline Blake
Adriana Bobrow
Sheree Bonsett
Meagan Bradley
Stefanie Broderick
Kendall Brown
Allison Brusher
Cindy Calvert
Hayes Chamoun
Sarah Chappell
Kimberly Colombrita
Loretta Coyne
Billie Dalglish
Rochelle Darman
Victoria Dawson
Michelle del Valle
Julie deRochemont
Marlyn Dickinson
Deborah Dunn
Liz Ferayorni
Kerry Ferguson
Deborah Flood
Cameron Foley
Katie Foreman
Elisha Frank

Kimberly Fundaro
Vanessa Gilyard
Katherine Godoy
Julie Goel
Sarah Goldfarb
Quinn Goodchild
Kristin Govoni
Blanca Granja
Katherine Guida
Nicole Hanaka
Heather Hancock
Wendy Harrigan
Stephanie Heckel
Erin Hemminger
Ann Herrick
Deborah Hohler
Michelle Hopkins
Coleen Hubbard
Dawn Huckestein
Linda Irwin
Betsy Jacaty
Kim Jaeger
Melissa Jakopin
Christin James
Tania Johansen
Nikol Johnson
Barbara Keith
Madeline Keller
Ayla Kirk
Peggy Kiser
Laura Kottke
Cristina Ladin
Suzanne Lang
Heather Larsen-Cheek
Stephanie Little
Jennifer Little-Kiss

Kate Lochrie
Erika Lucid
Lisa Malanowski
Alicia Malinowski
Beth Malkin
Amy Masri
Katie McCray
Tara McGinn
Cariann Moore
Heather Moraitis
Kimberly Morris
Ellen Murton
Angie Nelson
Erin O'Brien
Alexandra Moraitis Orman
Kandi Osman
Laura Overmyer
Jenny Palumbo
Kirsten Patterson
Tara Pasteur
Michelle Perry
Karen Petty
Elizabeth Pino
Angela Pohlman
Ann Powell
Randi Press
Lauren Presson
Sara Queen
Erin Rafter
Jennifer Ramach
Tracy Reese
Gina Ciolino Reynen
Christine Rickard
Audrey Ring
Jessica Rivera
Laura Rodgers

Mary Lou Ruderman
Angelika Schultze
Laura Scherwitz
Stacey Schwartz
Sara Sears
Marla Selva
Shelley Senecal
Janice Sham
Casey C. Simmons
Jennifer Snow
Vicki Strochak
Lori Ebinger Sullivan
Elizabeth Swann
Cindy Talley
Linda Tapp
Sarah Templeton
Lisa Trafford
Denise Treuil
Elissa Truman
Jessica Urbanski
Christine Von Wyl
Victoria Watson
Sarah Weitz
Ellen Whiteman
Jennifer Whittington
Amy Wylie

index

index

index

index

index

index

index

**JUNIOR LEAGUE OF
GREATER FORT LAUDERDALE**
Women building better communities

For additional copies of *Paradise Served*, please visit our
Web site, www.juniorleagueftl.org, or
telephone Junior League of Greater Fort Lauderdale
office at 954.462.1350.